MANAGING ONE'S SELF

BOOKS BY
JAMES GORDON GILKEY

MANAGING
ONE'S SELF

BY

JAMES GORDON GILKEY, M.A., D.D.

*Minister of the South Congregational Church
of Springfield, Massachusetts*

NEW YORK
THE MACMILLAN COMPANY
1932

SET UP BY BROWN BROTHERS LINOTYPERS
PRINTED IN THE UNITED STATES OF AMERICA
BY THE FERRIS PRINTING COMPANY

TO

WILLIAM GAY BALLANTINE

*Who has won admirers
in five generations*

FOREWORD

DWIGHT L. MOODY once made this significant confession: "I have had more trouble with myself than with any other person I know." If we are honest most of us must make the same admission. We have far greater difficulty managing ourselves than we do managing other people. Our most serious problems are personal.

This book discusses ten problems of this type, and describes the ways by which many individuals have solved them. As the reader will soon discover, the material in these chapters has been drawn from life rather than from imagination, and the suggestions as to the ways by which these problems can be solved have been tested repeatedly in actual experience. Those who would be interested to study other problems of this type are referred to two earlier volumes by the present writer.[1] It was the widespread interest these

[1] *Secrets of Effective Living,* and *Solving Life's Everyday Problems.*

earlier books aroused, particularly the fact that one of them was transcribed into Braille for the use of blind readers, which led to the preparation of this third volume.

The author has here made no attempt to conceal his interest in liberal religion, or his conviction that in modern Christian faith and the God to whom it points we find immense help in our struggle for self-mastery and self-development. Much of the material in these chapters might properly be called applied psychology. The author hopes even more of it might fairly be termed applied Christianity.

J. G. G.

April, 1932.

CONTENTS

MANAGING ONE'S SELF

CHAPTER I

LOCATING ONE'S SPIRITUAL BURDEN

I

A social worker in one of our large cities recently reported this incident. It concerns a child whose conduct problem had never been understood. "Martha appeared so stupid in school that her teacher thought she might be feeble-minded. She seldom spoke to the other children, and she rarely answered questions in class. The teacher reported that most of the time she 'merely sat and looked.' She was sent to a psychiatrist for examination, but to the teacher's surprise he insisted that her mind was normal and that the source of her difficulties lay elsewhere. A study of Martha's home finally disclosed the root of her trouble. Martha's parents had hoped their first child would be a boy, and the advent of unlucky Martha was a bitter disappointment. When the next baby proved to be a boy they were greatly elated, and promptly shoved Martha into an insignificant position in the family's life. The boy, Harry by name, was given precedence in everything, and the two children were compared in a way that was invariably disastrous for Martha's self-confidence. She would hear her mother say to visitors, 'Harry is a very bright child, but Martha is only ordinary. Harry has to help her with her lessons, and he does this remarkably well.' Or when anyone suggested that Martha run an errand or assume a responsibility the mother would exclaim, 'Let me get Harry for you. Martha could not possibly do that.' The result of this treatment was that Martha eventually lost all self-confidence and lapsed into silence and despair. Every effort she made toward self-expression was relentlessly crushed, and she was finally handicapped as tragically as if she had been bound in chains." [1]

What was the source of Martha's difficulties? Obviously it was no external burden. Martha's handicap was an inward burden—a fatal self-dis-

[1] See Karl De Schweinitz, *The Art of Helping People out of Trouble*, pp. 22-24.

trust. Only when that handicap was located and thrown aside could Martha become a normal child and make normal progress along life's road.

Similar situations appear frequently in the adult world. The puzzling actions of older people, actions ranging all the way from incomprehensible hours of silence to unexpected outbursts of temper, often prove to have their origin in secret burdens resting heavily on the mind and heart. If the individuals thus handicapped hope to attain a normal existence they must, like Martha, locate and throw off this unseen but fatal load. In their case, as in the case of unnumbered boys and girls, the first and most obvious steps toward a happy and an effective life are a heroic self-examination and a resolute self-culture.

> An enemy I had whose mien
> I stoutly strove to know,
> For hard he dogged my steps, unseen,
> Wherever I might go.
>
> My plans he balked, my aims he foiled,
> He blocked my onward way.
> When for some lofty goal I toiled
> He grimly said me nay.

"Come forth!" I cried, "lay bare thy guise!
The features I would see."
But always to my straining eyes
He dwelt in mystery.

One night I seized and held him fast,
The veil from him did draw,
I gazed upon his face at last . . .
And lo! myself I saw.[2]

Sometimes the adults who are thus burdened must have, if they are to locate and throw off their load, the help of an expert in psycho-analysis. Self-cure is frankly impossible, and the minor remedies suggested by well-meaning but uninformed friends are as ineffectual as household medicines in a case of typhoid. Consider this incident, reported in a current volume on personality problems. "A girl who came under our observation had exhibited from her seventh to her twentieth year an inexplicable fear of running water. Any splashing noise threw her into a state of almost uncontrollable excitement. She could recall no incident which would explain this strange and apparently irrational dread until one day an

[2] Edwin L. Sabin.

aunt whom she had not seen since babyhood paid her a visit. Something the aunt said wakened in her mind a vague memory, and then bit by bit a strange experience was recalled. When this girl was very small her mother had allowed her to spend a day in the country with this aunt. The mother had particularly cautioned the aunt not to let the child wander away into the woods as the child had done on several previous occasions. During the course of the day the aunt's attention was temporarily diverted, the little girl slipped away toward a near-by thicket, and when the terrified aunt finally located her again she was standing in a brook screaming with fear. Near by a waterfall was splashing vigorously, and the child fancied she was about to be swept over the edge and drowned. She begged her aunt not to disclose the fact she had run away, and the aunt, who felt that she herself was responsible for the unhappy episode, was only too glad to agree. Nothing was said at home about the incident, and in the course of time the memory of the experience gradually faded from the girl's mind. The only thing which remained was a persistent and apparently inexplicable dread of running water. When the incident was recalled and the complex situation thoroughly understood, the dread which had afflicted the young woman for so many years rapidly disappeared." [3]

Obviously such a case is too complicated and too individual in type to be dealt with in a simple way or helped by general advice. A girl with such a peculiar spiritual burden needs the assistance of an expert in emotional disorders. But there are, as any minister soon discovers, thousands of unhappy and ineffective individuals whose problem offers no such technical difficulties and who stand in no such need of specialized treatment. The tension and the failure of these people are traceable to simple, obvious, and pitifully familiar spiritual burdens. If these men and women will face themselves honestly and then deal with themselves heroically they can speedily locate their own handicap, gradually rid themselves of it, and then make normal progress toward happiness and achievement.

[3] See H. A. Overstreet, *About Ourselves,* p. 123.

II

One of the most common of the simple spiritual burdens is the habit of expecting recognition and commendation whenever we do anything praiseworthy. All of us build this habit unconsciously during childhood. We find ourselves surrounded by individuals who love us dearly and who watch with absorbed interest our development and our achievements. Knowing the stimulus which commendation and praise bring, these individuals remark constantly on the splendid progress we are making. This is the normal procedure in a home, a kindergarten, an elementary school, and a summer camp for children. If a youngster is persistently deprived of this encouragement and commendation he finds, as poor Martha found, that the development of a normal personality is almost impossible.

A serious difficulty arises, however, when we carry the habit of expecting praise and depending on praise from the world of childhood into the world of maturity. In the world of maturity praise is no longer dispensed with lavish hand, and if we demand that it shall be so dispensed we inevitably sentence ourselves to disappointment, self-distrust, and deepening bitterness toward other people. Here, for example, is a minister who delivers a carefully prepared and thoroughly rehearsed sermon, and who expects that at the close of the service his admiring parishioners will crowd about him congratulating him on his phenomenal pulpit ability. Here is a salesman who during a period of business depression sells far more than his share of the company's goods, and who for days thereafter scans the mails for the letter of congratulation he feels sure the president of the concern will write him. Here is a public-spirited individual who devises and carries through a project of obvious benefit for the community, and who then looks forward to the day when there will be a public recognition of his years of unselfish devotion to the common welfare. Or here are two parents who at the cost of heavy self-sacrifice give their children opportunities which they themselves never enjoyed, and who now wait expectantly for evidences of appreciation and gratitude on the part of the youngsters. In situations like these—painfully common, as we all realize—what usually happens? The minister's prize sermon evokes no comment whatever. The president of the company takes no notice of the salesman's achievement, the city awards no medal for the conspicuous public service of a tired and expectant citizen, and the children accept with bewildering nonchalance all that the self-forgetful parents do for them. How often, meeting these disappointments, older people lapse into disappointment, self-distrust, and bitter personal resentments! How often we hear them saying it was a sorry mistake to do so much for an unappreciative world! The source of all this wretchedness, this heavy burden of regret and chagrin, is plain to anyone who knows human nature. That source is the child's habit of expecting recognition and praise, a habit which has been transferred from the world of babyhood to the world of maturity.

The way of escape from this difficulty is obvious. We older people must compel ourselves to grow up. We must force ourselves to abandon the child's habit of depending on other people's compliments, and gradually build the adult's habit of depending on himself. Apparently Jesus had to learn this long, hard lesson. One of the most suggestive incidents recorded in the gospels [4] says that on a certain occasion Jesus healed ten lepers, but that only one of them showed any adequate evidence of appreciation and gratitude. How much of that story is fact and how much fiction no one knows. But whatever the percentage of fact the incident suggests a situation which Jesus, and every other adult before and since, encounters frequently. We are praised by only a few of the people we help. We are thanked for perhaps one kindness in ten. Evidently Jesus taught himself to continue living at his best in spite of these rebuffs. Each one of us must do the same thing. Once a man completes this self-discipline he makes a significant advance toward inward peace and emotional stability. He gains the power to do his duty whether he is praised for it or not. He ceases to depend on the commendation of other people and attains a priceless self-sufficiency.

During the early months of the World War the British troops stationed near Le Cateau were

[4] Luke xvii. 11-19.

obliged to make a quick retreat. There were only two roads leading back from the front, and unfortunately those roads crossed. At the crossing a scene of tragic confusion rapidly developed. Men and horses, motors and wagons, ambulances and trucks were hopelessly entangled. Worse still, the Germans discovered what was happening and directed a devastating fire on that crossroad. A wounded British officer, making his way painfully along one of those roads, saw what was going on, leaped on a horse, and began to direct traffic. All day he stayed at the crossroad, though two horses were killed under him and though he himself received several additional wounds. Only when the last men in the long columns had made their way safely through that danger point did he ride away on the third horse. Word of his heroism reached headquarters, and there was a rumor he was to receive the Victoria Cross as soon as his identity was established. But though he was repeatedly invited to appear at headquarters, and though it was known he was still living, he never made any effort to secure the high recognition which was due him. He had done his duty, and the realization he had done it was reward enough. He was not the type of man who lingers after a public performance hoping to overhear in the lobby a few words of praise! The strength and the stability of individuals like that British officer are rooted in a sturdy self-sufficiency. They have left the child's world and the child's attitude far behind, and have attained a man's estate.

III

Another spiritual burden which many people tug about with them is the habit of reviewing and regretting old decisions. Unfortunately many of the choices which we human beings must make are made in the dark. Try as we will, we cannot look more than a few steps down either of the alternative paths opening before us. How true this is of our choice of a life work! The college student who, as his senior year draws to an end, asks himself whether he ought to go into business or try his hand at teaching has no way of comparing his probable success in one career with his probable success in the other. He does not know what abilities he might develop as a business man, or what capacities he might reveal as a teacher. He certainly has no idea what personal weaknesses he might discover in himself in either career. He must stand at the parting of the ways, look forward into the dark, choose one of the two paths opening before him, and then plunge resolutely ahead.

The same situation emerges when two young people marry. They have no idea what experiences the coming years will bring, and no idea how they themselves will react to those experiences. Their marriage may prove the beginning of unimaginable happiness, or it may prove a colossal mistake. No one can say which. Everything connected with the venture is uncertain, and yet the two young people must make one decision or the other and then abide by the consequences.

If I leave all for thee wilt thou exchange
And be all to me? Shall I never miss
Home-talk and blessing, and the common kiss
That comes to each in turn; or count it strange
When I look up to drop on a new range
Of walls and floors, another home than this?
Yea, wilt thou fill that place by me which is
Filled by dead eyes, too tender to known change? [5]

[5] Elizabeth B. Browning.

No one can answer that girl's questions. But she must choose one of the two roads opening before her, and then follow it heroically to the end.

In this difficult situation many people fall into the fatal habit of reviewing and regretting vanished alternatives. If the road they are following becomes either steep or indistinct they instantly raise the question whether it is the right road. Should they have chosen the other career, married the other person, settled in California rather than in New England? Was the early training they gave the children the right one, and was their decision to send the youngsters away to boarding school wise? Here are questions which, as any doctor or minister can testify, have proved a nightmare to thousands of people. Here are doubts which promptly assail any individual who lets himself develop the fatal habit of resurrecting and reconsidering earlier decisions. The inner misery to which these questions and this practice lead sometimes becomes intolerable. People find themselves lying awake night after night asking whether everything in their career has been a mistake. What if their whole life has been a series of missteps in the dark?

How can we throw aside this burden of inward wretchedness? How can we develop a sane and a healthy attitude toward the uncertainties all of us must face? We may well begin our effort by reminding ourselves that we never know anything about the road we did *not* take. We fancy it was straight and smooth, and that it would have brought us speedily to the land of heart's desire. But this is, of course, sheer supposition. The road not taken may have been quite as steep and quite as circuitous as the road we actually followed. The college graduate who finds himself only moderately successful in business must not infer that he would have attained eminence had he tried teaching. The fact is he might have been even less impressive in a schoolroom than he is in a broker's office! The woman whose married life has been a succession of disappointments must not conclude that everything would have been happy had she accepted the other suitor or not risked marriage at all. There is every likelihood she would have found difficulties and heartaches, though admittedly of a different type, on either of those other roads. After all, it is a sorry blunder to wreck one's peace of mind over a supposition. It is a tragic mistake to let a guess wreck one's self-confidence and one's happiness.

Just as we know nothing about the road we did not take, so we know nothing about the future stages on the road we are now following. In our moments of despair we announce gloomily that our present road leads nowhere, that we are fools to continue following it, and that the only sensible thing is to get onto the right road—that is, the other road—without further delay. But here again we are making an unfounded assumption. We are assuming that our present road *is* the wrong road. What if this assumption is false? What if the next turn in the road will reveal the land of happiness and opportunity just ahead? What if the calamities we insist are waiting for us around the corner are not there at all?

> Some of your griefs you have cured
> And the worst you have always survived,
> But what agonies you have endured
> From the troubles that never arrived!

That familiar verse sums up the experience of unnumbered people. All of them were convinced their road was leading straight to ruin, and then the expected disaster quietly failed to materialize.

All this indicates the attitude we ought to take as we face the inevitable choices of life. When we reach a crossroad we should choose the path which, in the light of existing knowledge, seems the more promising. Then we should walk bravely and confidently down that path, making ourselves forget it ever began at a crossroad. Wherever the path leads we should follow it resolutely, heroically, and cheerfully, refusing to let other people entice us into discussions of alternative routes, and refusing to let our own moods of discouragement betray us into the fatal habit of inquiring what might have happened if . . . People with the habit of reviewing and regretting old decisions spend their years in an agony of ever-deepening self-distrust. Each new choice raises another question in their uncontrolled and increasingly apprehensive mind. People who make it a practice to forget a crossroad as soon as they walk past it discover in this habit a significant source of courage and power. They succeed in throwing off a spiritual burden which proves a fatal handicap to people of the opposite type.

IV

The other spiritual burden we mention is perhaps the most common and the most dangerous of all. It is the habit of rebelling against limitations which cannot be changed. Most of us begin life fancying we are in complete control of our own destiny, and believing we can make what we will out of ourselves. For perhaps fifteen years this happy confidence continues, and then we gradually discover permanent walls of limitation on this side and that. For one thing, we learn we were given a certain inheritance which—like a hand of cards—cannot be changed once the game begins. Whether we are satisfied with our physique or not, whether we are pleased with our native gifts or not, whether we have an appealing personality or not, is beside the point. We must take the cards originally dealt us and play them as well as we can. There is, unhappily, no way by which two-spots can be manipulated into aces, and no way by which an absent suit can be obligingly stuffed into the collection of cards we are holding.

The opportunities which come to us often prove equally uneven and equally disappointing. One sister in a family happens to meet the right man at the right time, and the succeeding years bring her marriage, children, and ever-deepening happiness. But the other sister, equally attractive and equally deserving, never finds her romance. Why? No one can explain. We can only say that opportunities, like native gifts, are distributed in strangely haphazard fashion. Meantime positive restrictions begin to make their embarrassing appearance in our little world. Grim walls of frustration rise silently but relentlessly around us, some of them erected by our own blundering hands and others by sheer coincidence. Eventually we find ourselves imprisoned, permanently deprived of the satisfactions which we see some of our friends enjoying. There is no adequate explanation for this bewildering situation. All we can say is that things have gone wrong. Mrs.

Browning described this experience in lines of
singular vividness.

> You who keep account
> Of crises and transitions in this life
> Set down the next time Nature says plain "No!"
> To some "Yes!" in you, and walks over you
> In gorgeous sweeps of scorn. We all begin
> By singing with the birds, and running fast
> With June days hand in hand. But once—for all—
> The birds will sing against us, and the sun
> Strike down upon us like a friend's sword caught
> By an enemy to slay us, while we read
> The dear name on the blade that bites at us.
> That's bitter and convincing! After that
> We seldom doubt that something in the large
> Smooth order of creation has gone wrong.

In this hard situation many people adopt an
attitude of bitter and irreconcilable protest. They
tell themselves day after day that life has treated
them with cruel unfairness, and they lie awake
night after night asking indignantly why they
were given so little when other people were given
so much. This attitude develops into the sorry
habit of rebelling violently and persistently against
life, a habit which reveals itself in one or more

of a dozen ways. Sometimes it emerges as self-
pity, sometimes as envy of those who are more
fortunate. Sometimes it appears as a curious loss
of self-confidence, sometimes as a steady weaken-
ing of ambition. In the more extreme cases it
leads to nervous or physical breakdown, or to
that most furious and futile protest of all—suicide. What is the source of this wide, dark stream
of misery? The habit of rebelling against limitations which cannot be changed.

How can we break this habit? We can certainly
tell ourselves, to begin with, that we are not
the only individuals who face disappointment
and restriction. Sooner or later, as Mrs. Browning
reminds us, everyone meets grim denials of his
desire. To imagine that we are the only people
who suffer frustration, that misfortune has chosen
us for its solitary victim, is to show an ignorance
of life which would be comic if it were not
tragic. We can also recall the fact that thousands
of people, facing as we do the gray walls of a
permanent limitation, have discovered inside those
walls both happiness and opportunity. Helen Keller never gained the priceless boon of sight, but a

day did come when in the exultation of inward triumph and astonishing outward achievement she cried, "To be blind is to know the joy of life!" Dr. Trudeau never regained the health and the opportunities which tuberculosis snatched from him, but—though imprisoned in the Adirondacks—he did find satisfaction, friendships, and innumerable chances to help others. How it heartens us to read the confession he made at the end of a hard but a singularly happy and effective life! "As I look back on my life tuberculosis looms up as an ever-present and relentless foe. It robbed me of my dear ones, and brought me my first great sorrows. It shattered my health when I was young and strong, and relegated me to this remote region where ever since I have seen its withering blight laid on those about me. And yet the struggle with tuberculosis has brought me experiences and left me recollections which I would not exchange for the wealth of the Indies." [6] There spoke a man who had discovered one of the most significant facts about life—the fact that restrictions, no matter how permanent

[6] Edward Livingston Trudeau, *An Autobiography,* p. 317.

or how inexplicable, cannot rob a man of the possibility of winning happiness, or take from him the chance to make himself a blessing to others.

Those of us who hold the Christian view of life go even further. We remind ourselves of the unfaltering love and the unfailing help of God—a love which enlarges its effort when darkness overwhelms us, and a help which comes in double measure during days of heartache and defeat. The old notion that God deliberately sends sorrow and suffering we now realize was utterly false. How could a God of love snatch sight from a child like Helen Keller, or deliberately thrust the germs of tuberculosis into the lungs of a young physician like Edward Trudeau? No human parent would show such cruelty. Can God be less kind than we are? Christians to-day are beginning to realize at last that the Biblical writers who attributed to God the misery of the human race were wholly mistaken. Here, as at so many other points, they were blindly repeating the blunders of an earlier generation.

If God is not responsible for the undeserved sufferings of men, who is? These sufferings are, as we now see clearly, traceable to the blind energies of Nature, energies which in these instances are turned against us by unhappy coincidence. It was tragic mischance that sent Helen Keller into the world with such a heavy handicap. It was sheer misfortune that lodged the germs of tuberculosis in Trudeau's lungs at the precise moment when a lowered physical vitality made him unable to resist their attack. When these fortuitous disasters take place what does God do? God does exactly what a human friend does. God makes every effort to lead us out of trouble—working persistently through our mind and the minds of other people to strengthen our courage, quicken our hope, and disclose to us pathways to victory. Why does God permit these disasters to happen in the first place? God's aim here, as far as our minds can fathom it, is to develop wise and kindly personalities, human beings dominated by the combination of intelligence and love. To produce individuals of this type, and to produce them by a slow and non-miraculous growth process rather than by quick manufacture, requires a special type of world. It is a world dominated by rigid laws,

a world in which human beings possess at least
some measure of free choice and creative power,
a world in which people are bound inextricably
together for weal or for woe, and a world in
which invisible and intangible personalities function through the physical mechanisms we call
bodies and brains. Only a world of this strange
and complex type could be an adequate training
school for character. Granted that such a world
has brought temporary suffering to unnumbered
individuals. For the race as a whole it has proved
a training school of surprising effectiveness, one
which has developed in an originally unimpressive
and unpromising humanity such priceless qualities
as intelligence, resourcefulness, endurance, and
kindness. If an observer could have seen the first
human beings as they emerged from the animal
world centuries ago he would never have dreamed
that the distant descendants of those human beings would reveal the virtues and the abilities
which are found everywhere to-day. You say such
a life scheme is fair for the individuals who
emerge late in the evolutionary process but bitterly cruel for primitive men? But suppose life is,

as millions of thoughtful people have believed, an endless thing. Suppose the growth process which we see beginning here continues not merely for the race as a whole but for every individual as well. Then the apparent element of injustice fades. In a world which offers immortality to everyone, a world which gives every individual the chance to live and grow forever, the Love which we Christians believe is at the heart of things is neither disproved by temporary disaster nor checkmated by tragic coincidence.

Once a man accepts this interpretation of life he gains the power to do a hard but immensely important thing—accept himself. He begins by accepting his inheritance, unpromising though it may seem. He accepts it and resolves that with God's help he will make all he can out of it. He then accepts his career, his home, his daily work, though all of them appear disappointing. He accepts them and looks confidently within them for the satisfactions and opportunities he knows God will put there for him. When, as the years pass, he finds barriers rising in his path he struggles heroically and persistently against them, realizing they are as much of a tragedy in God's sight as they are in his own, and remembering that God is constantly doing all that love can do to disclose to him a road around those barriers. If, in spite of all these efforts, his prison walls prove invincible he accepts without fear and without resentment the limited life forced upon him. He knows that God is his companion inside those grim barriers, and he realizes that God can be trusted to make even his prison a place of ever-growing happiness and ever-widening opportunity. What can take from such a man his inward composure and his outward triumph? Yielding to life rather than fighting against life, accepting permanent limitations rather than breaking one's heart struggling vainly against them—when we do these things we throw aside our heaviest spiritual burden and find within ourselves an abiding peace.

CHAPTER II

MASTERING AN INFERIORITY COMPLEX

I

HERE is a problem which concerns great numbers of young people. Recently a boy in one of the New England colleges wrote a friend this pitiful letter. "Two years ago I failed in some of my courses here, and I had to drop out of college for one year. My father was disgusted with my marks, told me he would not invest any more money in my education, and insisted that I take a business position. I went to work, hated the job, and finally made up my mind I would return to college even if I had to earn every penny of my way. This winter I have been back here, working day and night to maintain my marks and earn all my expenses. But my worst difficulty lies, I find, somewhere else. There is something in my mind which keeps throwing me back into a state of introspection and hopeless self-distrust. I am afraid of myself, afraid of other people, and afraid I may be compelled to do something in public. Sometimes I go almost frantic in my effort to conquer these feelings. I know they do not represent the truth, but I have come to the end of my own resources in struggling against them." [1] What was the problem this student was facing? A problem which perplexes hundreds of young people. The problem of mastering an inferiority complex.

Some individuals carry this difficulty from youth into maturity. Although they gain a certain amount of emotional poise, and although they fortify themselves with a certain record of achievement, they still find it hard—particularly in moments of sudden crisis—to generate an adequate self-confidence and assurance. Subjected to quick pressure or excessive strain they slump into cringing fear. All of us know middle-aged men and women who are terrified at the thought of expressing their opinions in public, and who deliberately stay away from a gathering if they learn there is a chance they may be called upon to answer ques-

---

[1] A personal letter addressed to the author.

tions. All of us know adults who, suddenly confronted by new problems or new responsibilities, suffer a pitiful spiritual collapse. They tell their friends they do not have enough intelligence to solve the new problems, enough strength to carry the new burdens, or enough courage to face the failure which will inevitably ensue if they are compelled to make the venture from which they so violently recoil. Sometimes these individuals never conquer this feeling of self-distrust and remain, to the end of their days, a serious problem for their friends. Sometimes, happily, they find the road to courage and eventually muster strength enough to carry their own burden. Dr. Fosdick gives this instance of a man who thus conquered an inferiority complex which had handicapped him from boyhood. "Recently a stranger with a sad record of self-distrust came to talk with me. When this man was a child his father used to beat him cruelly, and the shame of those thrashings cut deep into his sensitive soul. He developed a dangerous inferiority complex while still in his teens, and as he grew to manhood he always pictured himself as a complete failure. He went through college, married, and entered a business career, but he was always haunted by a feeling of personal inadequacy. Finally in despair he attempted suicide. Then one day, bewildered by his apparently unconquerable fear, he came to me. He was the saddest sight human eyes can look upon—a whipped and beaten man. Did he need to stay in that wretched condition? Certainly not! Together we found the way out. A few weeks ago I saw him again. He was on top of the world. He had found what the New Testament calls 'power to become.' "

But an inferiority complex does not always show itself as fear. Sometimes it dons a disguise and emerges as a trait of an entirely different type. Think of the hypersensitive people you know. Most of them are, in reality, victims of the sense of inferiority. Their hypersensitiveness is merely a symptom of this deeper difficulty. Secretly convinced they are not the equals of their associates, they are absurdly insistent that everyone in the vicinity give them special attention, recognition, and praise. The slightest criticism, no matter how kindly or how well deserved, rouses them to violent protest and long-continued resentment. Or consider the jealous people you know. Many of them are the unconscious victims of a sense of inferiority. Inwardly convinced they are less gifted than their rivals, these men and women develop a furious bitterness toward those who persistently outclass them. On the slightest provocation they criticize their competitors outrageously, and sit in glum silence while those competitors are being praised. Here we see an inferiority complex in disguise, masquerading as jealousy rather than disclosing itself in its normal form of self-distrust.

But the most curious manifestation of the sense of inferiority is the habit of boasting. Psychologists now agree that the extraordinary boasts we hear on the lips of little children are in reality attempts to compensate for an overwhelming feeling of personal insignificance. "My father's got more money than anybody in the world!" "I can kick the football over the schoolhouse!" "Don't you wish you could do what I can do?" Through these extravagant claims youngsters who sense all too clearly their actual limitations seek to give

themselves the comforting illusion of greatness.
Repeatedly we older people revert to this childish
attitude and practice. We tell friend wife what
extraordinary individuals we are, or we gather
the children about us to relate the magnificent
record we made in boyhood. As we brag and the
cowed members of the family listen, our crushing
sense of insignificance vanishes and we gain the
happy conviction we are in reality the extraordinary heroes our conceit and our imagination picture.

II

How can we master an inferiority complex?
The first step is fairly clear. Let us ask ourselves
whether our sense of incompetence tells us the
truth about ourselves, or whether—as in numberless instances—it is essentially misleading. In
the case of many individuals the sense of inferiority is thus traceable not to any actual deficiency
but rather to a faulty training received in childhood. Consider the man who came to interview
Dr. Fosdick. His sense of insignificance and his
resultant self-distrust were the after-effects of the

thrashings given him as a boy. His father, intending to discipline him but knowing nothing of the secret mechanisms of human emotion, beat the lad savagely. By doing this he did not succeed, as he expected, in making his son a fine man. Rather he succeeded in saddling his son with a sense of shame and self-distrust which almost wrecked the son's career. In this instance the boy's inferiority complex, though persistent and severe, gave the boy no reliable information about his own abilities or his own possibilities. All it did was prove that his father had made a sorry blunder years before.

Or consider a case of a different type. Here again the sense of inadequacy and the feeling of self-distrust, though immensely strong, were entirely misleading. Dr. Overstreet of the College of the City of New York reports this incident.[2] "A young man of twenty-eight, suffering from inordinate shyness, proved on examination to have a strange and a tragic history. His mother had stubbornly refused to let him take part in the normal activities and exploits of boyhood—base-

[2] See H. A. Overstreet, *About Ourselves*, p. 126.

ball, football, swimming and all the rest. She said he might get hurt. Thus a dread of these things was implanted in the boy's mind, and along with it a sense of shame that he could not do what the other lads of his age were doing. Naturally the boy repressed his dread and his shame, and this repression created within him the haunting fear that his comrades would think him a sissy. So the boy kept to himself, avoided contacts with other boys, and at twenty-eight found himself the sensitive, retiring, and ineffective person he was." What was the source of this man's self-distrust? Not any defect in his endowment. Rather a mistake his mother had made in his childhood training.

A faulty training in childhood is, however, only one of many sources from which a misleading sense of inferiority may spring. Consider the individuals who develop a tragic self-distrust because they demand the impossible from themselves. Here again we find a powerful inferiority complex, but here again it is one which is essentially untrustworthy. Some time ago a college girl came to me in great distress to describe the sorry record she was making in everything she attempted. She said she was sensitive and unsuccessful, and that during her school and college course she had won neither friends nor distinctions. What was the matter? Why was she haunted by self-distrust and ever-deepening misery? When she finished her story I asked her how old she was. She replied she had just passed her eighteenth birthday. Only eighteen, and yet disheartened about her record! Any older person could have told her the source of her wretchedness. She had lost perspective on herself and her situation. She was demanding from herself at eighteen qualities of character and a record of achievement which few people attain before twenty-eight or even thirty-eight. That girl's sense of discouragement and fear, though powerful and persistent, gave no real information about the girl's present gifts or future prospects. All it did was reveal the fact she was singularly impatient with herself.

Many older people repeat that girl's mistake. Many ministers expect themselves to preach as well at thirty as they will at fifty and then, discovering that their youthful sermons are frankly mediocre, secretly conclude that they are second-raters. Many business men expect themselves to make as extensive profits during a period of depression as they make during a period of prosperity and then, finding that in spite of all their effort their sales are dwindling steadily, jump to the conclusion that they themselves are either stupid or ineffective. Many parents expect themselves to do as much with an ordinary child as other parents do with a gifted child and then, discovering that their youngster achieves only an ordinary triumph, promptly accuse themselves of making blunders in their effort to train him. All these individuals are plagued by a sense of failure and a feeling of incompetence and yet, as any thoughtful person realizes, their self-distrust is wholly misleading. When you and I try to estimate the extent of our achievement and gauge the magnitude of our abilities we must always take into consideration the length of time we have been working, the nature of the situation in which we found ourselves when we began our efforts, and the number and the quality of the opportunities which life actually offered us. Only as we consider all these facts can we reach a fair verdict on our accomplishment, and escape a tragic but essentially unreliable despair.

There is still another source from which a misleading inferiority complex springs. Many individuals fail to realize what an immense rôle coincidence plays in human life, and stupidly hold themselves responsible for everything that happens to them. When a major disaster develops, or when a series of minor reverses crowds them into a subordinate position, they insist that they themselves must have blundered, and that their present misfortune is a proof they are incompetent. The result of this conviction is a deep and a lasting sense of inferiority, one which sooner or later creates serious difficulties. Yet in spite of its persistence and its power this feeling of inadequacy is entirely groundless. These individuals are not incompetent at all. They are merely victims of misfortune.

One of our playwrights has recently written an ingenious drama with alternative second acts. At the close of the first act the hero stands before a table in the center of the stage and as he leaves the room walks to the left of the table rather than to the right. This action, determined wholly by chance, prevents him from seeing a letter which had fallen to the floor at the right of the table. In the first of the alternative second acts the story of the hero's subsequent career is related. The audience sees him filling a relatively insignificant position and spending his days in relatively trivial undertakings. Then the hands of the clock are turned back, and once again the hero stands before the table at the center of the stage. This time, in leaving the room, he walks to the right of the table rather than to the left. On the floor he sees the letter, and learns from it a secret which opens the way to a career of major importance. This time he leaves the room to begin a life of thrilling achievement. His accomplishment in life hinged on a triviality—on walking to the right of the table rather than to the left at a moment of unrecognized crisis.

When we turn from the imaginary world of the theater to the actual world of daily experience we find that coincidence is quite as important as this play implies. Some individuals, meeting a succession of fortunate opportunities and coincidences, move forward with bewildering speed to positions of national or even international eminence. Other individuals, quite as intelligent and quite as deserving, meet a reverse at a critical moment and thereafter find it impossible to equal the achievement of their more fortunate contemporaries. What happens if a man is foolish enough to assume full responsibility for every occurrence that makes or mars his career? If he proves successful his habit of claiming full credit makes him intolerably conceited. If he proves unsuccessful this same habit develops within him a fatal, though a wholly unfounded, inferiority complex. He thinks of himself as a failure, though in reality he is not a failure at all. He is merely a victim of misfortune, one of the thousands of individuals who at the undetected crisis of their career blindly took the wrong turn.

All this suggests the first step in conquering an inferiority complex. Ask yourself frankly whether the inferiority complex is trustworthy. Does it tell the truth, the whole truth, and nothing but the truth? If on examination it proves to be the product of a faulty training received in childhood, or the product of impatient and extravagant demands which you make on yourself, or the product of mishaps for which you have stupidly assumed personal responsibility, then the sense of insignificance and personal inadequacy it creates should be quietly disregarded. You ought to pay as little attention to what it tells you as you would to the unfounded indictments and unjustified criticisms devised by an enemy. You ought to turn your mind in a new direction, adopt a new attitude toward yourself. You should assume you have as many abilities and as many possibilities as the people about you, and that—freed from the incubus of an unfounded self-distrust—you can make in the years ahead quite as gratifying a record as they can.

III

Suppose a man comes to this point in his thinking. Suppose he frees himself from false notions of his own limitations, and gains a reasonably accurate perspective on his own abilities and his own accomplishments. What are the further ways by which he can build up self-confidence, enlarge his ability to manage difficult situations effectively? There are several fairly obvious procedures all of us would do well to follow.

The first is this. Whenever we face a task which frightens us we should picture ourselves as succeeding in it rather than failing. This simple act of reassociating our ideas, coupling the thought of doing our work with the thought of doing it easily and well, is one of the most significant sources of new courage and power. Dr. J. A. Hadfield of King's College, London, gives this illustration.[3] "An aviator lost control of his plane, crashed to the ground, and was severely injured. After his recovery he found himself the victim of chronic fear and severe headaches induced by the fear. He was brought to us for treatment, hypnotized, and taken through the experience of falling. When he came to the moment of the crash he nearly leaped out of the bed in terror. The experience of losing control of the plane was evidently associated in his mind with

[3] See J. A. Hadfield, *Psychology and Morals,* p. 193.

the most extreme fear. Still keeping him under hypnosis, we associated that experience with an entirely new idea—the idea that the disaster was far in the past, that he had escaped death, and that there was now nothing to worry about. The next day we hypnotized him again, put him through the experience of the accident once more, and this time when the moment of the crash came we heard him say quietly, 'Well, there goes the ship! But *I'm* all right.' The experience of falling, once associated in his mind with abject terror, was now associated with confidence. As a result of this reassociation of ideas the man was permanently cured."

You and I, facing problems of self-distrust which are far less acute, can utilize a modified form of this same treatment. Are you terrified at the thought of speaking in public? The basis of your fear is probably your habit of associating the thought of a speech with the thought of nervousness, discomfort, and abject failure. The two sets of ideas are tied together in your mind, and when you draw forth one the other invariably follows. You can master your fear by the simple expedient of reassociating your ideas, tying the thought of making a speech with the thought of doing it easily and well. This is the way by which hundreds of people who must speak frequently reduce to a minimum the spiritual wear and tear incident on innumerable public appearances. "As a man thinketh in his heart so is he" [4]—those words have proved even truer than the man who originally wrote them imagined.

Another rule which has brought great help to some of us is this. As you struggle against self-distrust remind yourself that there is, somewhere within your personality at least one outstanding ability. You are not an underendowed individual who must live and work amid geniuses. You have your gifts quite as truly as other people have theirs. You can meet other people without secret self-distrust, and you can work beside them without embarrassed apologies. One of Mr. William Beebe's books contains this interesting paragraph about three of the well-known birds. [5] "Some day an epic will be written about the law of compen-

[4] Proverbs xxiii. 7.

[5] William Beebe, *The Arcturus Adventure,* p. 111.

sation, the most dramatic thing in Nature. The peacock, with his aristocratic, incomparable display of color, has only a wretched squawk of a voice. The nightingale, embodiment of glorious, soul-stirring song, has feathers of dullest russet and gray. And the albatross, master flyer, walks awkwardly along the sand, moving as though each step brought him acute agony." Mr. Beebe here gives a negative statement of the law of compensation, saying there is one thing each of these birds cannot do. He might have illustrated his principle in positive fashion, reminding us there is one thing each of these birds can do, and do with superlative skill. The peacock may fail in a singing contest, but on dress parade he has no rivals. The albatross may walk clumsily on the beach, but a few feet above the beach he is incomparable. The law of compensation gives each bird certain limitations, but also gives each bird at least one outstanding ability.

The same principle applies in the human realm. There may be many fine things you cannot do, but there is—in some realm—at least one fine thing you can do. Why are we so sure? Because

behind your life stand literally millions of forbears, each of whom contributed certain clearly
defined qualities to your complex inheritance.
From that vast array of ancestors you have certainly drawn at least one splendid gift. In the
complex mass of your inherited traits you can
certainly discover, if you look long enough and
hard enough, one quality which is capable of high
and significant development. By recalling these
facts hundreds of ordinary people have finally
broken the spell of self-distrust, emerged into the
sunshine of a normal and a happy self-confidence,
and gained the power not only to believe in their
own possibilities but also to locate and develop
their own hidden powers.

The third suggestion follows naturally from
the second. When you have found the one thing
you can do and do well, keep doing it until you
build within yourself a permanent sense of accomplishment. Once you gain that sense the
tragic feeling of inadequacy and inferiority will
never regain its dominion over you. You will
realize there is one fine thing which you have

done and which you can still do, and this realization will enable you to face life and people without apology and without fear. One of our social
workers reports an incident which illustrates this
principle vividly. "A woman who was friendless,
unhappy, and deeply depressed consulted us about
her personal problem. She said she found no pleas-
ure or satisfaction in her work. When asked what
that work was, she gave a long list of successive
occupations. She had been a cook, a lady's maid,
a clerk in a store, and an operator in a factory.
She had also been a teacher of Spanish, and when
she mentioned that task she showed her first and
her only evidence of enthusiasm. We surmised
that teaching was her gift, and on questioning
her learned that while she was teaching she found
genuine self-expression and gained a satisfying
sense of achievement. Around that one gift and
that one vital interest this woman's life and personality were deliberately rebuilt. We located a
few pupils for her, and as time went on their
number increased. At the end of a year in part-
time teaching this woman was a more stable and

a more contented individual than she had ever been before." [6]

What brought this significant change? The sense of achievement. With that sense even an ordinary individual can speedily generate enough courage and self-confidence to face life bravely and happily. Without that sense even a gifted individual sinks into despair and misery, as the records of most long-term prisoners prove. It makes little difference what the particular act is by which we create within ourselves this highly essential feeling of accomplishment. One man may generate that feeling by preaching sermons, another by repairing the automobile which no one else in the service station can put in running order, and still another by playing an unusually clever game of contract bridge. But our own accomplishment, whatever it is, brings us the priceless conviction there is something we can do and do well. That conviction in turn breaks down our feeling of self-distrust, and prevents the development of an inferiority complex. Years ago

[6] See Karl De Schweinitz, *The Art of Helping People out of Trouble,* p. 212.

Emerson sensed this truth and stated it in one of his most memorable epigrams—"Every man's task is his life-preserver."

Does Christianity make any contribution to the solution of this problem of self-distrust? The final rule for conquering an inferiority complex utilizes one of the great principles enunciated by Jesus. The next time you are beset by fears of present insignificance and future failure remind yourself that life constantly offers each of us, no matter what his situation may be, the chance to find enduring happiness. It offers us this chance by putting us close to people who need our help. If we take our thoughts off ourselves and begin to think and work for other people we find, as Jesus did, a joy which no disaster or disappointment can ever take away. You and I do not need to be rich, famous, or even highly gifted to find the sense of significance which we crave, and the feeling of happiness which inevitably flows from it. These things are available to us no matter how small our income is, how limited our friendships are, and how few our native abilities may be. Happiness and satisfaction invariably come to us as we forget ourselves and spend our energies meeting the needs of others. "He that loseth his life for my sake shall find it" [7]—hundreds of people who were once threatened by self-pity, self-distrust, and a deepening sense of failure have found this path from secret misery to a new life of contentment. In losing their life in the service of others they have found that life again, but found it glorified by a new richness and transformed by a new splendor.

Some years ago *The Survey* published the story of a woman who has demonstrated the truth of this familiar Christian teaching. As a child of ten she was placed in an orphanage in a mid-western State. She was sickly, ill-tempered, ugly to look at, and—worst of all—a hunchback. By a curious coincidence her parents, both dead, had named her Mercy Goodfaith. Some months after her arrival in this orphanage a childless couple came there seeking a girl for adoption. To the surprise of the matron the wife explained she wanted a child whom no one else would take. Mercy Goodfaith was called into the room, and when this

[7] Matthew xvi. 25.

woman saw her twisted back, her scowling face, and her embittered eyes she said quietly, "That's the girl I've come for." For the next twenty years this foster mother did everything in her power to teach Mercy that in spite of her handicaps a life of happiness and satisfaction could be hers. It lay open before her in the needs of other people, and in her power to forget herself in meeting those needs.

Some years later one of the men who were inspecting the orphanages in that same State mailed this report to his superior: "I have just been visiting the Home in such-and-such a town. The house is exquisitely clean, and the twenty children there seem unusually happy. I had supper with them to-night, and afterward we all went into the living-room to sing. One of the older girls played the organ, and the other youngsters clustered about the matron. Two small girls sat on one arm of her chair, and two on the other. She held the smallest of the children in her lap, and I noticed that one of the big boys who was sitting on the floor took the hem of her dress in his hand and stroked it gently all the time we were there. The children adore that woman. She is a hunchback named Mercy Goodfaith. Her features are very plain, but you forget all about them when you see the light in her eyes." "He that loseth his life for my sake shall find it." Jesus discovered the surest road to happiness and courage.

CHAPTER III

LIMITING THE LOAD ON ONE'S MIND

I

SOME time ago I received this letter from a woman who was heavily burdened by the sense of strain. "I once spent several weeks in a sanitarium where the doctor used to give a talk to his patients every Sunday night. He would say to us, 'Almost everyone who comes here suffering from nervous exhaustion claims he is completely run down. As a matter of fact none of you are run down. All of you are wound up. Until I can persuade you to unwind and run down I can do nothing for you.' His whole course of treatment was built around the idea of inward relaxation, and he was highly successful when he could persuade his patients actually to relax. My trouble now is that I can find no time for this sort of thing. I resolve to get myself inwardly quiet, and I just begin to gain a certain degree of poise, when an interruption comes. The telephone or the door bell rings, and there stands someone who is determined to make me subscribe to a magazine, purchase Christmas seals, buy soap, give money to charity, or bake a cake for the next church fair. I think I could manage life and eventually throw off my sense of strain and weariness were it not for these incessant interruptions and continual demands. Our little community, as you doubtless realize, is sadly overorganized. Even the children here are determined to start new clubs and raise money for something. If you could tell me how to live a busy life and still keep inwardly at peace I should be deeply grateful."

The problem this woman describes is familiar to all of us. We too find ourselves in a world of constant interruptions and unending demands. We realize, as she did, that we ought to keep at the center of our being a core of quietness. Otherwise how can we live happily and work effectively? The question is how we can maintain this inner serenity in an environment of uproar and confusion. A few individuals solve the problem in an obvious way. At frequent intervals they leave their community, and in the seclusion of Florida, California, or a hotel at Atlantic City escape from the tumult of their usual surroundings and gradually regain their emotional balance. Other people remain in their community, but at times resolutely withdraw from all its activities. They accept no more responsibilities, serve on no more committees, absent themselves from all public gatherings, and even disconnect their door bell and their telephone. Now at last they can have a few days of peace!

But for most of us, as for the woman who wrote the letter we just quoted, these obvious solutions of the problem are impossible. Much as we should enjoy running away for frequent rest periods in distant localities we cannot do so. Our work holds us relentlessly and continuously where we are. Neither can we withdraw from the ventures and the burdens of our community's life. The nature of our work compels us to maintain friendly relations with other people, no matter what the cost may be. This means that when our friends ask us to serve on their committee or assist them in raising the budget of their favorite charity we can do nothing but smile wearily and consent. How can we expect other people to assist us in our projects if we refuse to assist them in theirs? Thus we finally find ourselves face to face with the very problem which that letter so vividly described. How can we remain in a distracted and distracting world, carry our full share of its burdens, and still maintain within ourselves the sense of quietness and poise?

Some of us are convinced that this problem, though apparently insoluble, can be solved. We feel that the secret lies in deliberately limiting the load that falls on the mind. If you and I permit all the burdens and all the anxieties which emerge in our world to crowd in upon us we soon find ourselves bewildered and overwhelmed. But if we learn to restrict our mental and spiritual load, adjusting the burden we assume to the strength we possess, we discover we can not only make our way through days of tumult and heavy pressure but also maintain an unfaltering inward poise. What now are the concrete ways by which we can thus limit the load on the mind? How can we restrict our burdens until a life of sustained calm is substituted for a life of tension, overstrain, and persistent weariness? Here are four simple rules which have proved of great practical value.

II

The first is obvious. Never permit yourself to carry two sets of burdens at the same time. Numberless people fall into this fatal habit, and as a result they eventually find themselves so overwrought and so distracted that they become a serious problem not only to themselves but to their friends as well. Some of these individuals attempt to drag about with them not only the single disappointment of to-day but also the accumulated disappointments of a thousand yesterdays. Talk with these people and they will relate to you not only the tale of their most recent misfortune but also the serial story of the successive misfortunes of the last ten, twenty, or even fifty years. Obviously such men and women are carrying two sets of burdens at the same time—the burden of to-day's disappointment and the burden of yesterday's as well. Such individuals can never gain inward peace. Their spirit is hopelessly overloaded, cluttered with an array of unhappy recollections which should have been laid aside years ago.

Meantime other people make the equally serious blunder of carrying about with them the innumerable responsibilities of a long future as well as the single responsibility of the present. Talk with them and they will tell you not only of the work they must do to-day but also of the interminable succession of duties waiting for them in the future. Such men and women are mentally burdened by the many decisions of many to-morrows as well as by the single decision of to-day. They are spiritually wearied by the anxieties of a thousand coming hours as well as by the one anxiety of the present moment. One of the Pilgrims who sailed on the *Mayflower* in 1620 was a man of this type. Just before the ship left Holland Robert Cushman wrote a friend, "If we ever make a plantation in the new world God works a miracle! Specially considering how scant we shall be of victuals, and most of all ununited amongst ourselves. If I should write you of all the things which promiscuously forerun our ruin I should overcharge my weak head and grieve your tender heart. Only this I pray you. Prepare for evil tidings of us every day. Pray for us instantly. I see not in reason how we shall escape." No wonder poor Cushman had lost his composure! His mind was burdened with a load no mind was ever intended to carry—the single trouble of the present, and in addition the innumerable troubles of a long future.

Suppose this habit of carrying yesterday, to-day, and to-morrow at the same time is the source of your sense of strain. How can you break this habit? Remind yourself, to begin with, that the past is utterly beyond your control. Not all the tears, prayers, and regrets on earth can change the slightest part of it. Therefore let the past go! Whether it was a success or a failure, a record of wisdom or of stupid blunders, a tale of noble virtues or of ugly sins, let it go. Regretting the past will never change the past. Mourning over old sins and ancient mistakes will never bring the chance to correct them. Therefore let the past slip away, never to be recalled. Then, as you turn untrammeled toward the present, remind yourself that no matter how busy life may become you will never have to face more than one problem at a time. Moments always approach us in single file, never in a crowd. In the one moment immediately before us only one problem can possibly present itself to us, only one responsibility can possibly devolve upon us. There may be innumerable problems lurking in the vicinity, and there may be unnumbered responsibilities waiting to drop upon us in sequence. But down the narrow defile we call Time problems and responsibilities invariably come in single file. By learning to manage our duties one by one we gain the power to manage our entire life, no matter how complicated our life may be. By learning to focus our mind on the one problem of the moment, and then shift our focused attention onto the problem of the next moment as the next moment brings that problem, we master not only the art of achievement but also the art of living without a sense of strain.

III

The second rule for limiting the load on the mind is equally simple and equally helpful. Stop watching for the results of your work. Did you ever realize how many people fall into this habit, and how serious the consequences are? Numberless men and women, finishing a given undertaking, instantly look about to discover what the attitude of the general public is, and to learn what the results of their achievement will probably be. Have other people noticed how well they did? Was there an adequate appreciation of their unusual technique? Will they receive the recognition, the commendation, and the promotion they deserve? Then, disastrously enough, these men and women cast sidelong glances at their rivals. Are those secretly detested competitors receiving undue attention and favor? Do they win greater returns on the expenditure of an equal amount of thought and energy? These are the mental habits and the spiritual attitudes of hundreds of the people about us. Can such individuals ever attain inward peace? Not possibly. Their mind is overloaded—burdened with concern over the work that must be done, and also burdened with concern over what people will say about that work when it is finished. Rufus Jones writes, "There

are many individuals to-day who are working constantly for the good of others but who, in spite
of all their altruism, never gain the peace of God.
They are in a frequent state of nerves, busy here
and there, rushing about perplexed and weary,
fussy and irritable. The trouble with these people
is that they never succeed in forgetting themselves.
They are always watching for the results of their
work, always wondering what other people will
say about it, always showing an absurd touchiness
over honor and recognition. Such people cannot
possibly gain inward peace. They have the very
attitudes which frustrate peace and drive quietness
from the heart."

What ought our attitude to be? All of us must
learn to do our best, and then let results take care
of themselves. This is not an easy lesson or a
simple accomplishment, yet it is the price of abiding peace. After we have done our best can we
actually trust gratifying results to follow? The
testimony of human experience is plain. If we do
our work—whatever it is—supremely well, recognition and promotion are inevitable. We do not
have to watch for them, struggle for them, or

even make hints about them. Like the tide they inevitably flow toward us when their time comes. Success, in any endeavor, is not an aim. It is a result, the result of work done well over a long period of time. If our work is of the right quality we can, when the work is finished, sit back and wait. Life can be trusted to make the seed which we have planted spring up and grow—first the blade, then the ear, then the full corn in the ear. Like the farmer in Jesus' parable [1] we can sleep and rise during this growing process and show little anxiety about the eventual harvest. The earth brings forth fruit "of herself," and the farmer does not have to worry himself into a breakdown wondering whether the seed will actually change into ears of slowly ripening corn.

What about the comments of the general public during this waiting period? We may school ourselves not to fret about results, but what about the comments, insinuations, criticisms, and stupidly inaccurate verdicts other people pass on us and our endeavors? Let us all remember that no matter what we do or how we do it some people

[1] Mark iv. 26-28.

are sure to criticize us. A few other people are sure to commend us, and still other people—perhaps the majority—are sure to miss the significance of our aims and our efforts. Under these circumstances the wise thing is to disregard completely the comments of the ignorant, the envious, and the malicious. We can, and we should, give careful consideration to the suggestions made by those who love us, those who understand our aims and our difficulties, and those who appreciate the efforts we are making. But the remarks of uninformed outsiders should be quietly and steadily ignored. Only when we deliberately place our feelings beyond the reach of incompetent critics and jealous rivals can we attain the inward quietness we seek.

You may get through the years but your march
    will be slow
If you listen to all that is said as you go;
You'll be worried and troubled and kept in a stew
For talkative folks must have something to do,
    And so they will talk.

If you're quiet and modest it will be presumed
That your humble position is slyly assumed;

You're a wolf in sheep's clothing, or just a plain
     fool,
But don't get excited, keep perfectly cool,
  And let people talk.

If you show resolution and boldness of heart,
A slight inclination to take your own part,
Some people will say you're conceited and vain,
But keep right on working and never explain,
  For folks will still talk.

The best rule to follow is: Do as you please.
Then your mind will be quiet, your heart be at
     ease.
We all can be sure of some praise, some abuse,
So don't listen for comments, it's a plan not to use,
  For people will talk.[2]

IV

Another rule many individuals have found immensely helpful as they seek inward peace is this.
Stop trying to explain life. Take life, unpromising though it is, and look confidently within it
for opportunity and satisfaction. Some time ago
an elderly man who had been the victim of an
almost incredible succession of tragedies sub-

[2] Samuel Dodge in *The World's Famous Short Poems*,
p. 65.

mitted this question to Dr. Cadman. "I am seventy-four years of age. I find myself unable to answer the following question. Can you answer it for me? In 1895 my wife, stricken with melancholia, took her own life. In 1901 my eldest son died of a fever. In 1920 my eldest daughter, temporarily out of her mind with acute depression, shot herself. In 1924 my only living son and his two children were burned to death in their own home. My question can be summed up in one word—Why?" Could Dr. Cadman or any one else give a convincing answer to that question? Never. To that bewildered inquirer who had suffered so bitterly life was, and would always be, an insoluble riddle. His only chance of gaining inward peace was to stop trying to explain life, and to begin trying to make something fine out of life—poor and broken though life was.

The tragic situation which emerged in this man's world emerges in less acute form in everyone's world. Sooner or later all of us encounter disasters, restrictions, and disappointments which we are unable to explain. Why were we given an inheritance which creates so much trouble for us?

Why were we permitted in youth to make blunders which have brought innumerable difficulties into these later years? Why are we relentlessly kept in a world of small opportunities and satisfactions when there is every indication we are intelligent enough and skillful enough to fill a larger place? Eventually all of us find ourselves asking one or more of these questions. It is significant that almost the last words attributed to Jesus were, "My God, why?" [3] Jesus could not find in his day the full answer to the riddle of life. No one of us can find the full answer to that riddle even now. If we hope to gain even a measure of inward quietness we must do what Jesus and many other people before and since Jesus have done. We must regard life not as a problem to be solved but as a succession of concrete situations to be met—met bravely, confidently, hopefully, and with no trace of bitterness or self-pity.

If a man faces life in this fashion can he hope to find—sometime and somewhere—the opportunities and satisfactions he craves? The best answer to that question is the answer given by

[3] Mark xv. 34.

history. Thousands of individuals, utterly unable to explain why their situation was what it was, finally succeeded in finding within their bleak world chances at happiness and achievement which most contemporary observers would have insisted were not there. Two generations ago a crippled, misshapen baby was born in Breslau, Germany. Both the child's father and grandfather had been victims of spinal trouble, and their weakness was passed on to this boy. As the years passed, one tragedy after another befell him. While he was still a baby his mother died, and long before he reached boyhood it became evident that his deformity could never be corrected. He learned that, to the end of his days, he would be a hunchback, and that he would suffer almost constant physical pain. But deformity was not his only handicap. Just as he was finishing his studies at the local university he was told that the authorities had become suspicious of his alleged radicalism, and that it would be wise for him to leave Germany at once. Off he went to Switzerland— crippled, friendless, distrusted, desperately poor. In 1889 he reached New York, traveling in the steerage of an immigrant liner. Could this young man explain life? Not possibly. Could he figure out why he had been born with a twisted spine, why pain was his constant companion, why he had been maneuvered out of his own country, and why he remained poor and friendless? Neither he nor any one else could answer those questions. But fortunately for the world Charles Steinmetz did not spend his time trying to answer them. With hope in his eyes and confidence in his heart he limped down the gangplank and entered his new world—America. What did he make of himself? Eventually he became one of the world's leaders in electrical research and engineering. When he died in 1923 scientists from every land paid him their tribute of gratitude. One admirer wrote, "This deformed hunchback had the mind of an angel and the soul of a seer." [4] Explain life? Steinmetz never could do that. But he could take life, believe in life, and finally win from life opportunities and satisfactions which men of a less courageous spirit would have insisted did not exist.

[4] See Archer Wallace, *Overcoming Handicaps*, pp. 13-21.

Take what life gives, O heart of mine,
And build your house of happiness!
Perchance some have been given more
But others have been given less.
The treasure lying in your hands
That seems so paltry to your view
Another builder, looking on,
Would give his heart to have from you.
Tomorrow Time's relentless stream
May sweep what you now have away,
O take what life has given, and build
Your house of happiness today! [5]

V

The final rule for limiting the load on one's mind is one which has meaning only for those who accept as true the Christian belief in a God of love. This final rule is simple but immensely helpful. Leave with God his share of the responsibility for your career.

What is it a Christian believes about God's care? A Christian believes that God is quite as deeply concerned over the task of building a better world, and over the task of using each of us to the full in that endeavor, as we are. A Christian

[5] B. G. Williams.

is convinced that God shares with us this hope,
this effort, and this responsibility. Before you and
I were here at all God was at work shaping a
nobler world, and using men and women like ourselves to help Him in the process. Long after
we are gone He will still be at work on this vast
undertaking. All God asks us to do to-day is live
steadily at our best, meeting life's varied problems
and successive responsibilities with our keenest
intelligence and our bravest courage. When this
is done our duty is discharged and God's duty
begins. It is His task to make the seed we have
planted spring up and grow. It is His task to
give us the opportunities we deserve, the work
we have fitted ourselves to do, and the training
we need for the greater responsibilities He may
put upon us in the future. It is His task to lead
us elsewhere when He needs us and wants us
elsewhere, and His task to open the doors which
must be opened before we can leave our present
career and begin the new one. Our responsibility
is to do the best we can in the immediate situation
in which we find ourselves. God's responsibility
is to make the most of that best of ours, and

then either keep us in our present place or bring us to a new place in which our best will be of greater service to Him and His cause.

Unfortunately many people who count themselves Christians never recognize this sharp division of responsibility. They try to carry the full burden themselves, laboriously lifting their share of the load and God's share too. These individuals feel they must do their best, and also that they must make sure their work has the proper recognition and the right results. They feel they must toil steadily at their present task, and also that they must locate unaided another task when this one is finished. They feel they must struggle to rescue themselves from peril and difficulty and, if they are finally to be rescued, do all the thinking, planning, and working themselves. What happens when we take this distorted view of life? Quietness and confidence invariably desert us. We lose the priceless inward poise disclosed by the men and women who meet life in a different spirit. "Thou wilt keep him in perfect peace whose mind is stayed *on Thee*." [6] In that sugges-

[6] Isaiah xxvi. 3.

tion and the habit to which it leads, these men and women have found the secret of unfailing inward calm.

One of the chapters of Dr. Grenfell's autobiography [7] contains a vivid account of the most disconcerting single experience in the Doctor's long and hazardous career. He had been summoned to a village on the Labrador coast to perform an emergency operation. In order to reach the village as quickly as possible he risked driving across a wide river which seemed safely frozen. But part way across the river the ice suddenly gave way, and Dr. Grenfell and his dog team were plunged into the freezing water. Eventually he pulled himself and the dogs onto a huge cake of drifting ice, and then sat there helplessly while the current swept the ice cake and its shivering cargo toward the distant Atlantic. There were no dwellings for miles along that river, and Dr. Grenfell's only hope of rescue was that some of the fishermen who lived at the very mouth of the stream would happen to see him and his dogs as they drifted out into the Atlantic the follow-

[7] W. T. Grenfell, *A Labrador Doctor,* Chapter XVIII.

ing day. Here is the doctor's own account of the hours that followed.

"Night found me ten miles on my seaward voyage. I had killed three of my dogs, stripped off their skins, and wrapped their fur about me as a coat. Their bodies I piled up to make a windbreak on the ice. At intervals I took off my clothes, wrung them out, swung them in the wind, and then put them on again, hoping that the heat of my body would dry them. Forcing my biggest dog to lie down I cuddled close to him, drew the improvised dog-skin rug over me, and eventually dropped to sleep. The hand that was against the dog stayed warm, but the other was soon frozen. About midnight I awoke shivering. The moon was just rising, and the wind and current were sweeping me steadily toward the open sea. But somehow my faith was unshaken. After all, it seemed the natural thing for a Labrador doctor to be drifting toward the portal of death on a half-frozen stream. And quite unbidden the words of a hymn I had learned in boyhood began running through my mind:

My God and Father, while I stray
Far from my home on life's rough way
O teach me from my heart to say,
   Thy will be done!"

There is the final secret of gaining inward peace. It is to leave with God God's share of the load.

CHAPTER IV

CONTROLLING ONE'S MOODS

I

Why is self-control such a problem for us all? Because within each one of us is a strange jumble of tendencies drawn from a long line of varied ancestors. To bring a fine and enduring order out of that chaos is no easy undertaking. Professor James Harvey Robinson gives this account of the modern man's situation. "Underlying the mind of a man today there are four distinct layers —the animal mind, the savage mind, the child mind, and the traditional mind. All of us are animals, and we can never cease to be. For half a million or a million years our ancestors lived in savagery, and the savage mind is ever with us. All of us were children at our most impressionable age, and we can never get over the effects of that. Finally we were born into an elaborate civilization, the constant pressure of which we can never escape. Thus in all our thinking we have at least three unsympathetic companions looking on with jealous impatience—an apish progenitor, a savage, and a peevish baby. Most of us also have a fourth companion—a Greek philosopher, an ancient mystic, or a mediaeval monk. At any moment we may find ourselves overtaken by a warm sense of camaraderie for any or all of these ancient pals, and we may experience a curious sense of relief as we yield and disport ourselves with them as of yore. It is on this strange, fourfold foundation that we raise the structure of life today. How insecure the foundation is such things as depression, anger, fear, or even ordinary irritation speedily reveal." [1] When we consider these facts we realize that the surprising thing about people is not that they lose control of themselves occasionally. The surprising thing is that they have themselves under control most of the time.

But this complex racial inheritance is only the beginning of our difficulties. Behind each one of us stand six immediate ancestors—two parents and four grandparents—who passed on to us a strange

[1] See J. H. Robinson, *The Mind in the Making*, pp. 65-67.

medley of family traits. Nature usually brings together as mates individuals who are curiously unlike, and then passes on to the children the mingled and contradictory qualities of both parents. If all our six immediate ancestors had been of the same type our problem of self-control would be relatively simple. Had the extremes of our inheritance canceled each other out and left us with a simple collection of conventional qualities the task of managing ourselves would not be difficult. But all six of our immediate ancestors were different in type, and from the six there came to us a curious jumble of mutually contradictory traits. Father's conscientiousness and Mother's dread of responsibility are both present in us, and one day we reveal the first quality and the next day the second. The hot temper of one grandfather and the hypersensitiveness of the other combine to create for us a peculiarly difficult personal problem. The saintliness of one grandmother and the anything-but-saintliness of the other were both passed on to us, and instead of counteracting each other emerge alternately. Some Sundays nothing could keep us away from church, and other Sundays nothing could drag us there! Mastering one's self when so many discordant inner forces are forever threatening mutiny is no easy undertaking. In one of Mrs. Humphrey Ward's novels one character says to another, "I thought, Elizabeth, you would understand me." Her friend answers, "That, Lucy, is something only your Maker could do. And sometimes God Himself must be puzzled to account for you!" You and I often feel that way about our friends. The likelihood is they often feel that way about us.

On this composite foundation and from these jumbled materials each of us tries to build a unified, stable, and attractive self. That venture continues through many years, and several successive periods are clearly discernible in the long effort. During the first ten or fifteen years of life we gradually bring our animal inheritance, our savage inheritance, and our childish inheritance fairly well under control. We learn not to scratch, not to fight, and not to be terrified by strange sights and sounds. We learn to make ourselves reasonably acceptable members of a modern and an adult society. Only on rare occasions and under the stress of peculiar emotions do the traits which characterized the animal world, the savage world, or the child world make their appearance. During the next ten or fifteen years we try, if we take this matter of self-control seriously, to reduce to ordered effectiveness the chaotic inheritance derived from our parents and grandparents. We note the faults and failings of each of these six immediate ancestors and quietly resolve that in our case these mistakes will not be repeated. We locate the fragmentary virtues given us by these individuals, and make every effort to develop and perfect these powers, reorganizing our personality around what fine traits and what better-than-average abilities we possess. Thus by the time we reach the late twenties or the early thirties we have made a fair start on the long and difficult task of shaping a consistent and satisfying personality. What is the problem which then emerges? Sometimes we call it the problem of controlling our moods. Sometimes we call it the problem of living steadily at our best. Sometimes we call it the problem of keeping the better part

of our nature constantly in evidence, and the
unfortunate part of our nature permanently out
of sight. But whatever name we give the problem,
the problem is familiar to us all. It is the task
which every mature person faces every day of his
life. It is the task of holding himself resolutely
on his own highest level.

II

Suppose a man is willing to make a serious
effort to live at his best. How can he conquer
fluctuations of feeling? How can he control his
moods? There are two preliminary disciplines he
may well undertake at once.

To begin with, he should study himself carefully and learn just when his self-mastery is liable
to break down. Each of us has a breaking point,
and the man who knows exactly where his lies
gains an immense advantage in the struggle for a
steady life. He knows what situations and tensions to avoid, and he realizes that if these situations and tensions develop unexpectedly he must
then guard himself with special care. It is interesting to study different people and note what

their breaking points are. Some individuals can endure prolonged physical and spiritual exertion but speedily go to pieces under criticism. Splendidly able to work long and hard when there are emergencies to meet and crises to manage, they lose their self-control completely if they are forced to stop working and listen to a relentless analysis of their methods and their mistakes. Such a situation precipitates in them a mood of indignation, resentment, bitterness, and—in the end—self-distrust. Here lies, apparently, the weakness of many ministers. Recently one of the professors in an influential seminary made the significant statement that it is almost impossible to teach middle-aged preachers how to improve their sermons. The moment analysis is attempted and criticism offered, even in the kindliest and most tactful way, most of these men rush violently to their own defense. They insist that the sermon the professor is tearing to pieces was of almost unimaginable benefit to their parishioners. Here we see men who can endure the steady strain of a difficult career but who cannot endure the quick and severe tension of unexpected criticism. Subjected to that tension their self-control snaps and they slip into a mood of angry resentment and stubborn self-satisfaction which is unworthy of them and their profession.

Other people, able to endure criticism, lose control of themselves when they are compelled to have face-to-face dealings with the one person they particularly dislike. In all other situations, and in contact with all other men and women, these individuals can be trusted to conduct themselves in commendable fashion. But bring them into the same room with the one person who, for some inexplicable reason, rouses their worst traits, and presently there will be thunder on the left, lightning on the right, and murky weather everywhere. The venerable joke about collisions between son-in-law and mother-in-law has its origin in this familiar situation. Mother-in-law proves a thoroughly acceptable visitor in many homes, but *not* in this one. Son-in-law proves able to evoke admiration from many people, but *not* from this incomprehensible woman. Bring these two individuals together, and within thirty minutes each will be dangerously near the boiling point. If you and I are in earnest about controlling our moods and living steadily at our best, here is a discipline which we may well undertake at once. Let us study ourselves until we know exactly when our self-mastery is likely to break down. Being fore-warned we shall be forearmed, and the likelihood of a sudden and unhappy regression to the animal level or the child level will be proportionately reduced.

The other preliminary discipline is similar in type. Let us study ourselves until we know what we are likely to do when our self-control breaks down. Here again different people reveal curious differences. They have not only varying breaking points but also varying behavior patterns when the break comes. Some individuals, for example, begin to talk vociferously the moment their self-mastery gives way. They splutter to anyone or everyone in the vicinity or, failing to locate a listener, orate to the furniture or write their best friend an interminable letter. Other people, los-ing control of themselves, take the opposite course. They lapse into prolonged silence, and for hours or even days scarcely speak to the other members of their family. Anyone who is unfortunate enough to live in the vicinity is advised by a sign language far more revealing than words that a cosmic disaster has recently taken place. Still other people, subjected to severe strain, indulge in an orgy of secret self-pity and bitterness. Perhaps this is the most common procedure among well-bred groups. These men and women do not tell their troubles to the neighbors, nor do they make the members of their own family miserable by prolonged and ominous silences. Instead they carry the full burden of suffering themselves, stubbornly refusing to let it drop for even a moment. How heavy that burden finally becomes outsiders seldom surmise.

The chances are that you and I will act in one of these three ways the next time our self-control breaks down. We should study our past record with the utmost care until we know which of these courses of action we are likely to follow. Why is this self-knowledge of value? Because it will enable us to recognize our own danger signals, detect the advent of a dangerous mood, and then make swift plans for our own deliverance. To understand when an enemy is likely to make his attack, to know in advance what form that attack will probably assume, and to realize what the indications of its onset are, is to have a battle half won before the battle begins. Why do we not apply this obvious truth of military tactics to the familiar problem of our battle with ourselves?

III

Suppose, now, an unpredicted and unpredictable mischance upsets our normal self-mastery. Suppose we find ourselves slipping down to a lower level of thought and action. How can we conquer our mood? How can we pull ourselves back to the high level on which we usually live, and on which we are particularly anxious to live in this emergency? If you study moods carefully you will discover they are as varied in type as diseases, and that the methods we must use in combating them are as varied as the treatments employed by physicians.

Some moods can be mastered by the simple expedient of ignoring them. This is probably the best way to manage the mood of irritation against circumstance and resentment against people which is so familiar to us all. If we make the mistake of brooding over petty annoyances, and the mistake of recalling personal antagonisms, a mood of bitterness will soon fasten itself upon us. It may settle on us so firmly that days or even weeks will pass before we regain a normal attitude toward life and people. When we miss the train we tried to catch, when we return to the office in the evening only to discover that our stenographer left the wrong letter for us to sign, or when we find that one of our friends is making inane and cruel remarks about our work, then we should force a smile, make ourselves ignore our sense of irritation, and disregard completely the feeling of anger and resentment which rises within us. Most of us give our children careful training in this regard. When we see them losing their temper because their mittens are misplaced, or because a schoolmate has made fun of them at the wrong time, we say to them, "Snap out of it!" Would that someone could give us the same wise counsel when we indulge in similar exhibitions of childishness!

This is also the best way to manage ordinary moods of weariness and discouragement. Granted that the sense of physical exhaustion and spiritual fag is often traceable to serious disorders, and that in these instances the attempt to "brace up" is not only ineffectual but dangerous. We should also realize that many moods of weariness and despair are insignificant and untrustworthy things, and that we can conquer them by the simple expedient of refusing to take them seriously. Many brave people force themselves to begin working when it is desperately hard to make the first effort, and then presently succeed in throwing off their inertia and equaling their normal record of achievement. Much of the world's daily accomplishment must be credited to heroic men and women who make themselves go to the office when they would vastly prefer to spend the day in bed, or who compel themselves to finish a hard task even though they feel desperately tired long before the work is done.

A second type of mood is conquered in an entirely different way—by deliberately shifting the focus of the attention. This is the way by which some of us master many moods of tension, fear, and self-distrust. We deliberately turn our mind from the situation which is breaking down our morale, put our thought on something entirely new, and by that momentary escape from our burden and our perplexity gain the power to ward off a mood which otherwise might overwhelm us. Recently a business woman in New York City, employed in one of the office buildings overlooking the Hudson, made this interesting confession. "When things begin to happen thick and fast, when I find the feeling of tension and self-distrust coming over me, and when it begins to seem as if I couldn't stand the strain another minute, I go over to the window and look as far as I can up the Hudson. Then I realize that a God who is big enough to make a world like that is big enough to take care of me." Her words give a vivid picture of the conquest of a mood by a deliberate shift of the focus of attention. Perhaps this is the experience which underlies a striking verse in one of the Psalms—"I will lift up mine eyes unto the hills, from whence cometh my help." [2] Perhaps

[2] Psalm cxxi. 1.

this poet of long ago had discovered that by taking his eyes from the problems and perplexities which surrounded him, and by gazing for a moment at the quiet hills and the overarching sky, he could regain his normal poise and perspective, and then throw off his mood of weariness and despair.

Here, undoubtedly, lies the explanation of the benefit which comes to us when, in the midst of an exhausting day, we drop our burden temporarily and find something to laugh about. Such an action removes us in spirit from our wearing situation, gives the mind a new object of attention, and then sends us back to our work inwardly refreshed. In a recent biography of Lincoln this significant incident is recorded. "One day during the most crucial period of the Civil War Lincoln called a cabinet meeting, and announced that business of the utmost importance would be considered. When his advisers gathered he entered the room and glanced swiftly at the circle of anxious faces. Then he quietly picked up a book by Artemus Ward and began to read aloud one of its most uproarious chapters. By the time he had finished the chapter the indignation of the cabinet members was painfully apparent. What did Lincoln mean by bringing busy men there to hear a funny story? Finally Lincoln laid the book down and sighed deeply. 'Gentlemen,' he said, 'why don't you laugh? With the fearful strain that is on me night and day I should die if I did not laugh occasionally. You need this medicine as much as I.' Then he turned to his tall hat on the table, and drew from it what Secretary Stanton later described as 'a little white paper.' It was the first draft of the Emancipation Proclamation."

There is a third type of mood which must be conquered in still another way. When we find emerging within us, as all of us occasionally do, the sudden desire to abandon our ideals and give vent to our passions, we can usually conquer the mood by recalling the confidence other people have in us. The thought of our friends and the high expectations they have for us will, in emergencies of this type, almost invariably give us the extra bit of energy we need for the reëstablishment of our crumbling morale. Consider these three incidents, and note the common psychological factor in them.

The first took place in the darkest days of the American Revolution. During the cruel winter at Valley Forge, when many of his troops threatened to desert, Washington shrewdly arranged a review of his ill-clad, rebellious regiments. As a particularly haggard and resentful group stood at attention before him he drew himself up proudly and exclaimed, "I have great confidence in the men of Connecticut!" What was the appeal he made to those dispirited men? What was the thought he thrust into their minds to counteract the thought of disloyalty and rebellion?

The second incident was reported at the close of the World War. When a certain American regiment returned from France after months of weary delay, the father of one of the lieutenants had a long and frank talk with his son. At the close he asked the young man directly whether he kept a clean moral record during the tedious weeks after the Armistice. The lieutenant gazed at his father in astonishment. "Of course I did!" he exclaimed. "There are some things men with our name can be trusted to do." What was the power which had bolstered that young man's idealism during a highly difficult period of moral tension? What was the source of the energy which had enabled him to fight down a mood that had overwhelmed many of his companions?

The third incident was related by an acrobat who for many years provided one of the thrills at a well-known circus. After describing the feat which he and his partner performed night after night, he added this interesting comment. "More than once we lost our nerve just before the act began. We told each other we wouldn't try the big stunt at that performance. But then, when the band began to play our entrance number and we saw the crowd waiting to see us perform, our nerve always came back. We would walk out in the ring, listen to the applause, and then risk our necks as we had promised."

How different these three scenes! Continental soldiers trying to retain their loyalty to Washington and his cause, a young lieutenant fighting the battle with a perennial temptation, two acrobats plucking up courage to do what they had agreed to do in a circus—there seems no element of connection between the three situations. Yet anyone who knows human nature realizes that the same spiritual energy was at work in all three cases. It was the thought of other people's confidence and other people's high expectations which enabled these men to fight and master their dangerous mood. No one can compute the number of men who, day after day, hold themselves steadily at their own best by thinking of their friends, remembering the confidence their friends have in them, and resolving secretly they will never disappoint that trust.

There is one other type of mood we must mention, the bleakest and most dangerous of all. It is the mood of utter dissatisfaction and despair which occasionally sweeps over us, usually at the times when we are overtired. In these moments the work we are doing suddenly loses its accustomed significance and interest, the future seems utterly dark, and we ourselves crave only the chance to run away. How can we conquer this mood?

Many people succeed in mastering it by delib-

erately thinking of God—His wisdom, His power,
His unfailing care. Even if they have mismanaged
their responsibilities He has not mismanaged His.
Even if they have come to the end of their
resources He has not come to the end of His.
They can cast their burden on Him, rely on His
greatness, rest in His unfaltering care. In the end
He will bring things out right. "The eternal God
is thy refuge: underneath thee are the everlasting
arms." [3] Who can compute the amount of strength
and courage those words have given mankind?
"Cast thy burden on the Lord: He shall sustain
thee." [4] Numberless men and women, bewildered
and discouraged by situations they cannot manage, have fought off the mood of utter despair by
repeating this old verse. It is the thought of
God—His wisdom, His power, His unfailing care
—which gives them strength enough to regain
their normal self-control.

Suppose we do cast our burden on the Lord.
Suppose we do rest on the Everlasting Arms. What
will happen? Will God really take care of us?

The next time those questions trouble you

[3] Deuteronomy xxxiii. 27.
[4] Psalm lv. 22.

remind yourself that God's care of human beings is much like the care we parents give our children. Obviously we cannot protect our boys and girls against all possibility of disaster. No matter how ingeniously and how persistently we try to guard the children, accidents may invade our defense and bring sudden and undeserved tragedy. Neither can we promise the children that all their undertakings will meet with success. The situation in which they work is infinitely complicated, and even though they display great wisdom and we reveal unfailing love the uncontrollable elements in life may conspire to thwart their efforts and our hopes. The most we parents can do is surround the children with our love, and offer them day by day the resources of our wisdom, our loyalty, and our encouragement. Sometimes, thanks to their effort and ours, the children attain the goals they hope to reach. Sometimes, in spite of all that they and we do, disastrous coincidence brings suffering to them and us. If tragedy thus develops what attitude do we parents reveal? We gather the boys and girls even more closely to us in tenderness and affection, we offer them even more fully the resources we possess, and we do all that love can do to devise new opportunities and satisfactions to replace those which mischance and disaster have swept away. Throughout the years, no matter what experiences life brings, our children can always be sure of one thing. It is our love, a love which never fails.

Many of us picture God's love and care in the same way. God does not guarantee that we will be preserved from all possibility of suffering and disaster. In a world like ours, dominated by rigid processes of Nature, how could God make such a promise? Neither does God guarantee that all our ventures, even those which most clearly deserve success, will succeed. When the uncontrollable factors of coincidence and human free will are operating everywhere about us, how could God assure us that none of our undertakings will miscarry? He and we are at work in a world which is crammed with dangers and packed with risks. What God does promise His children is this. Whenever men live steadily at their best God surrounds them with His resources of wisdom, strength, and high incentive. Moment by moment

He brings from those resources His help. The wisdom God gives emerges in men's minds as a new thought, a fresh insight, a reawakened memory. From those sources springs the new knowledge for which men pray. The strength God provides emerges in men's hearts as the sudden realization they are not alone in their efforts for the good. From that source springs the new courage and the new endurance which men seek. The high incentive God brings emerges in men's souls as a new ideal for themselves and their community. From that secret source flows the determination which gradually transforms a hundred unhappy situations. Granted that all of us meet many unexpected and undeserved reverses. Like children who are strengthened by the love and help of their parents, we find ourselves inwardly renewed by the nearness and the tenderness of God. Our external situation remains exactly what it was before, but our attitude toward that situation is profoundly altered. We realize that God's resources are ours, that He will give us power to try again, and that under His guidance and with His sustaining strength we shall finally locate a path to victory. This is the faith of a Christian, and this is the method by which a Christian conquers the mood of despair. He reminds himself that no matter what happens there is one thing he can always be sure of. It is the love of God, a love which never fails.

CHAPTER V

LEARNING TO WORK UNDER PRESSURE

I

ONE of our essayists recenty drew this picture of the modern business man. "Business is no longer part of American life: it *is* American life. The average business man now devotes twenty-four hours a day to it. Before daybreak an alarm-clock wrests him from his fitful slumbers. He gulps down business news along with his eggs and coffee. He plans business on his way to the office, and spends his morning reading business, talking business, and dictating business. He keeps a business engagement for lunch, and afterward rushes back to the office where all the afternoon he routes himself, schedules himself, and dispatches himself as though he were an express train. After every one else has gone home he wraps up his business and carries it home in a brief-case. He arrives late, sits down to dinner, and throughout the meal stares glassily into space. He is conjuring up phantoms of business failure. Suddenly the telephone rings. It is a business acquaintance who wants advice on the stock-market. Ten minutes later the poor man returns to the table too overwrought to eat, and begins to pour out his troubles to his wife. He spends the evening studying budgets, reports, and trade journals. Finally he turns wearily to bed. Bed is, he has learned from long experience, the best place in which to worry out a solution to business problems." Suppose we abandon the sarcasm and study this man sympathetically. What is his problem? One of the most familiar, and also one of the most perplexing, in the world. It is the problem of learning to work under pressure.

Sooner or later all of us meet this problem. The type of pressure varies with different individuals, but in every life stress and strain eventually make their appearance. In some cases the element of pressure is created by the accumulated weight of many different problems and many varied responsibilities. This is true of the men who occupy key positions in the business and industrial world, and of the men who fill political positions of immense responsibility. Who can gauge, for example, the pressure that falls on a President of the United States or a Prime Minister of England? In the case of other people the element of strain is produced by a steady succession of trivial personal demands. This is the situation we find in the life of a doctor, a nurse, a social worker, or a minister. All day long disheartened and bewildered men and women turn to these individuals for help. A moment finally comes when these individuals feel they cannot interview another person, answer another telephone call, or see another visitor. Recently an overtired social worker exclaimed to a friend, "My job is to listen all day to a succession of hard-luck stories, offer encouragement and advice to an endless stream of disheartened individuals. When five o'clock approaches it seems as if I couldn't bear to see another person coming up the stairs." How many people know that woman's feeling and share her predicament!

For still another group the element of tension

is created by internal rather than external strains. These men and women may be relieved from the necessity of thinking and planning for others, and they may be shielded from the approach of needy individuals. But deep within their own hearts they carry a load of anxiety which at times threatens to overwhelm them. Study the letter which John Bunyan wrote shortly after he was confined in Bedford Jail, and note the type of pressure which was falling upon him. "The parting from my wife and children hath been as the pulling of the flesh from the bone; and that not only because I am somewhat too fond of these great mercies, but also because I have often brought to my mind the thought of the hardships, miseries, and wants my poor family will be like to meet should I be taken from them. Especially my poor blind child, who lies nearer my heart than all else. The thought of what my blind one may undergo almost breaks my heart to pieces." It was under that intense inward pressure that Bunyan began to write *Pilgrim's Progress*. It is under a pressure equally great that many of our contemporaries are trying to do their work to-day.

It is an open secret that many individuals never learn how to manage these tensions. As long as no real pressure falls on them they handle their responsibilities fairly well and make a reasonable success of their personal relationships. But the moment a serious strain develops, either in the outer or the inner world, these individuals promptly go to pieces. Some of them burst into a torrent of excited speech. Such a woman once confessed to her minister, "I am one of those unfortunate individuals who, when things go wrong, talk and talk and talk. Perhaps you know the type." All of us know the type. Its habitat, like that of the grass, is the entire world. Other people, compelled to work under pressure, gradually but steadily lose effectiveness. Hundreds of business men who make a fine record during a period of prosperity reveal a steadily dwindling courage and a steadily declining resourcefulness during a period of depression. Hundreds of ministers, subjected to a week of unusual strain, reveal on Sunday the fact that under pressure they cannot produce an interesting sermon. Still other individuals, subjected to hardship and tension, collapse entirely. Some suffer a breakdown, and a few take refuge in suicide. The protracted business depression which began in 1929 proved that great numbers of our contemporaries are wholly unable to endure the pressure of serious and long-continued anxiety. One of the insurance companies in Connecticut published in 1931 a significant statement in reference to the marked increase in the suicide rate during 1929 and 1930. In 1926, out of the total amount paid by this company in death claims, only about two per cent represented payments in which suicide was involved. But by the end of 1931 that figure had jumped to eight per cent, and in the case of a rival company it had increased to twelve per cent. The individuals who thus ended their own careers were people who had never learned to solve what is undoubtedly one of life's most obvious problems. They had never taught themselves to work under pressure.

Suppose you are one of the many persons who face this problem to-day. How can you manage the incessant strains that fall upon you? How can you maintain your normal poise and your normal efficiency in an atmosphere of tension and an environment of anxiety?

II

Before we attempt to answer those questions there is one fact which should be stated clearly. There are many people who are themselves to blame for the excessive pressure falling upon them. They have assumed too many responsibilities and undertaken too many ventures. The resultant sense of weariness and confusion under which they labor is not due to circumstance, the organization of modern life, or the contrariness of things in general. It is due to the blunders of these people themselves.

In such cases the solution of the problem of overstrain is obvious. These men and women must abandon the attempt to accept all the invitations which reach them, abandon the attempt to assume all the responsibilities which the community seeks to pile upon them, and abandon the attempt to climb to higher and higher financial and social levels. To counsel such deliberate retrenchment may seem strange doctrine in a

country which is committed to the "bigger and
better" policy. But however unfamiliar the doctrine of controlled ambition, is it not demonstrably
sound? Every American city has its quota of
young people who are now living under terrific
financial and emotional strain for the simple reason that they have tried to organize their life on
too elaborate a scale. They now find it impossible to maintain the schedule of payments on the
new radio, the new furniture, the new car, and
the new suburban property which they recklessly
purchased on an installment plan. Life resolves
itself into the bitter effort to make a three-thou-
sand-dollar income cover a four-thousand-dollar
expenditure. Every American city also has its
quota of older people who are worn out, physically and nervously, by the hectic effort to keep
the pace set by their younger and more energetic
neighbors. Each year these middle-aged men and
women push themselves to earn more money, do
more work, and carry more burdens. Life thus
becomes a frantic struggle to keep innumerable
wheels in motion, and each year set up still more
wheels. What is the wisdom all these overambi-

tious individuals need to hear? Wisdom given the world centuries ago—"A man's life consisteth not in the abundance of things which he possesseth." [1] Better to enjoy happiness and good health in a little world than to endure incessant weariness and suffer ultimate collapse in a big one. Better to have peace of mind in a cottage than suffer constant anxiety trying to pay the installments on a palace.

III

Suppose, in spite of all your efforts at intelligent self-limitation, a distinct element of pressure remains in your world. Suppose you find that circumstance compels you to carry not only your own burdens but the burdens of an ever-increasing number of friends. Suppose the nature of your work subjects you to an unusual number of irritations, annoyances, anxieties, and interruptions. How can you teach yourself to work quietly and effectively in such a situation?

You might begin by locating and eliminating the needless mental strains. Some mental strains

[1] Luke xii. 15.

are permanent and inescapable, but others are essentially unnecessary. The most familiar of the needless strains is the one created by the notion that we can and should please everybody. Most of us, particularly if we received during childhood the conventional training in good manners, reached maturity believing we could satisfy everybody and offend nobody. That became our aim—to make everyone an admirer. We fancied that if our actions were wise they would provoke no hostile comment, that if our decisions were intelligent all our associates would agree with them, and that if our statements were accurate everyone would immediately and enthusiastically applaud them. But presently, to our surprise and our chagrin, we learned that this is not the case. We found there is no possible way by which we can please everybody. No matter how wise our actions, how intelligent our decisions, or how accurate our statements, an appreciable number of people question what we have done and said, and a small group shows distinct hostility toward us. Some of these critical individuals prove, on careful examination, to be actuated by envy or malice.

Others prove to be ignorant of our problems and our objectives, and still others prove to be dominated by an irrational and inexplicable prejudice against us. If a man is foolish enough to believe that he can please everyone, and ignorant enough to fancy that if he does what is right he will please everyone, he subjects himself to an intense and an incessant—though an utterly needless— mental strain. There is no possible way by which he can give universal satisfaction or win universal acclaim. He must do what seems to him, at the moment, the wisest and best thing he can do, and then take with equanimity both extravagant praise and extravagant blame. If he develops this attitude and builds this habit he will find the strain of life perceptibly diminished, and his ability to work under pressure appreciably enlarged.

Another needless mental strain is produced by the familiar but erroneous belief that we can make all our ventures succeed, and if any of them fail we ourselves are in some way responsible. Here again most of us, particularly if we had conscientious and solicitous parents, reached maturity with a theory and an ideal which could not stand searching analysis. We were eager to win success, we were confident we could win success, and we were convinced that if our undertakings miscarried we ourselves were thereby proved at fault. Like primitive men we argued forward from intelligent planning and hard work to ultimate achievement, and backward from failure to either laziness or stupidity. But as the years pass what do most of us discover? We learn that thousands of individuals who deserve success suffer heart-breaking defeat, and that thousands of well-conceived and ably managed enterprises end in abject disaster. Why? Because only a few of the many factors essential for success are under the control of the people who are trying to succeed. A business venture which, by all the laws of probability, should show a profit may be wrecked by an unpredictable change in public taste or the sudden disappearance of a certain type of raw material. A sermon which, because of its inherent truth and the skill of its construction, should be of profound help to those who hear it may fail completely. The sudden sound of rain on the church roof distracts the attention of the congregation and leaves the minister preaching bravely but uselessly to individuals who are wondering how they will get home without being drenched. If a man is foolish enough to believe that he can succeed in everything he undertakes, and ignorant enough to fancy that if he does his work intelligently and well he will invariably succeed, he subjects himself to an intense and incessant—though an utterly needless—mental strain. He must learn to do his best, and then with a certain aloofness of spirit take what comes. If you study the men and women who possess the ability to work easily and effectively you will find that they trace much of their skill to their habit of dodging the needless mental strains we have just described. They have taught themselves to live above praise and above blame, and they have deliberately put their feelings beyond the reach of an occasional disaster.

Another self-discipline which those of us who must live and work under pressure may well undertake is this. Let us school ourselves to concentrate all our attention and all our energy on the one task immediately before us, and then when that task is finished move all our attention and all our energy to the task next in line. Unfortunately many people never acquire this skill. If during a given hour they have five things to do they scatter their attention and their energy over all five during the entire period. Suppose, at the moment, they are working on task number three. They make the mistake of sending stray thoughts backward to tasks one and two. Did they do the first correctly? Was the second completed when they turned from it? Then, with equal damage to themselves, they dispatch another portion of their attention and their energy forward to tasks four and five. Apparently the fourth task will be exhausting. Will they be too tired to do it well? Obviously the fifth task will require a great amount of time. What if they should run short of time before that task is finished? These are the mental habits of thousands of our contemporaries. No wonder such individuals find it difficult to work under pressure! When responsibilities multiply and advance in swift succession the attention of these people scatters and their energy spreads thin. Presently they find themselves in that state of confused ineffectiveness which we

note in little children when several demands are
made upon them at the same time. The nervousness, indecision, and lack of power which these
people reveal, and the dull headache which most
of them speedily develop, are conclusive evidence
they have never learned one of life's most important lessons—the lesson of controlling and con-
centrating the attention.

How do we gain the power of mental concen-
tration? There is only one way—by determined
and long-continued practice. Fortunately for us
all we can begin practicing at any time and in any
place. Here and now we can start thrusting out
of the mind regrets over yesterday and fears for
to-morrow. Here and now we can take our
thoughts off the comments other people make
about us and the criticisms they pass upon our
work. Here and now we can undertake the venture of stifling our worry over the situations we
cannot control, and conquering our anxiety about
the friends who live at a distance. In any or all
of these familiar ways we can practice focusing
our attention on the one task immediately before
us, and through this practice—continued patiently

for days and weeks and years—gradually gain the power to concentrate all our energy on a single problem or a single responsibility. You and I do not need an extraordinary mind in order to live quietly, easily, and effectively. All we need is an ordinary mind that can be focused. In one of the laboratories in Washington is a burning-glass which measures three feet across. When it is hung in the window it converges thirty-six inches of ordinary sunshine in one tiny point of flaming radiance. That point is hotter than a blowtorch, so hot that it will melt its way through a steel plate as easily as a heated needle will burn a hole through tissue paper. Three feet of common sunshine, but common sunshine that has been perfectly focused.[2] An ordinary mind, disciplined to concentrated effort, is capable of achievements quite as impressive.

There is a third suggestion which many of us have found helpful. When the pressure falling on us begins to seem unendurable let us give ourselves a few moments of complete quietness. In that brief interval, like the interval between suc-

[2] Reported by Roger W. Babson.

cessive plays in a game of football, we can accumulate a surprising amount of strength, resilience, perspective, and courage. It is usually the tired athlete who is injured in a football game. It is usually the tired individual who collapses under pressure. Dr. Hadfield of London gives this admirable advice. "There are ample reserves of power at the disposal of each of us, but we must have moments of perfect mental quiet if we are to draw upon them. Life, like music, has its rhythm of silence as well as its rhythm of sound. The habit of resting between successive tasks gives us these priceless periods of quiet, and enables us to take the strength which is waiting for us. This habit does not mean, of course, that we must withdraw from life in monastic retreat. Rather it means that, in the midst of pressing duties, we must withdraw in spirit from the turmoil, and during a moment or two of complete inner silence gain the calm we so deeply need." [3]

You say you could never grow quiet amid the tumult in which you must live and work? But other people, situated quite as unfavorably as you are, have learned to do this. Some of them give

[3] See J. A. Hadfield, *The Psychology of Power*, p. 47.

themselves saving periods of silence by going alone and sitting with their eyes closed, their hands relaxed, and their tired mind deliberately put off duty. Was this what Jesus meant when he spoke of going into one's inner chamber, closing the door, praying to the Father who is in secret, and then discovering that this Father gives a new strength which is presently obvious to everyone? Other people, still more adept in the art of resting, gain this same inner quietness and renewal by the act of transferring their attention from the problem which is perplexing them to a new and inspiring thought. These individuals do not need to leave their familiar surroundings, even to retire into an inner chamber. Their own mind, perfectly disciplined, gives them entrance to a world of silence and splendor. In one of his most suggestive poems Matthew Arnold described a man with this ability. The poem is entitled "East London." [4]

'Twas August, and the fierce sun overhead
Smote on the squalid streets of Bethnal Green,
And the pale weaver, through his windows seen
In Spitalfields, looked thrice dispirited.

[4] From Matthew Arnold, *Early Poems, Narrative Poems and Sonnets.* By permission of The Macmillan Company, publishers.

I met a preacher there I knew, and said,
"Ill and overworked, how fare you in this scene?"
"Bravely," said he, "for I of late have been
Much cheered with thoughts of Christ, the Living
    Bread."

"Much cheered *with thoughts. . . .*" It was not a change of environment which brought this man the quietness and refreshment he needed. Rather it was a group of new thoughts, thoughts held steadily in the focus of attention while the drab external world remained as noisy, as sordid, as uninspiring as it had been all summer.

The final suggestion may possibly be the most helpful of all. If you want to learn to live and work under pressure stop fearing your own life. In numberless cases it is secret fear which precipitates tension, anxiety, and ultimate collapse. Many of the people about us are desperately afraid—afraid they will not be able to do the work expected of them, afraid they will go to pieces if the pressure continues, afraid they are doomed to an ultimate and an ignominious defeat. If this fear could be swept away, if these people could be convinced they can not only manage life but manage it easily, their problem would be solved. Have we any idea how such self-distrust can be conquered? Many people have conquered it by the simple expedient of studying the records other men and women have made, and by reminding themselves that what other people have done they themselves can do. Until one has actually tried this method of mastering fear he has little idea how effective it is.

Some ninety years ago a boy named George Matheson was born in Glasgow.[5] While he was still a baby he developed a serious infection at the back of his eyes, and the oculists his mother consulted told her he would always have trouble with his sight. For seventeen years the boy, his parents, and his teachers fought the slowly encroaching darkness. The boy was given the best glasses money could buy, at school he was assigned a seat near the window, and after school his lessons were read to him. But the light steadily faded, and when Matheson was part way through Glasgow University complete and permanent darkness descended. Blind for life, and

[5] See Archer Wallace, *Stories of Grit*, p. 1-10.

blind while still in his teens—what ample reason that boy had to fear his own life!

But with a courage beyond all praise Matheson resolved he would finish his college course and then prepare for an active career. In 1861 he graduated from Glasgow University with honors in philosophy, and then began to study for the ministry. The record of his achievements as a minister, first in a small church in Glasgow and then in one of the largest churches in Edinburgh, almost passes belief. He was forced to memorize every part of every service he conducted, as well as prepare the sermon and the prayer. In addition he did in Edinburgh the parish work required by a church with no less than eighteen hundred members. In odd moments he found time to write innumerable lectures and articles, and complete no less than twelve books. His daily schedule, followed faithfully until he died at the age of sixty-four, shames many of us who are constantly complaining about overwork. After breakfast each morning someone read Matheson his mail, and he immediately dictated an answer to each letter. It was a point of honor with him to reply to a correspondent the very day the correspondent's inquiry reached him. When the letters were finished, Matheson had someone read him the more important items in the daily paper. After he had caught up with the news he turned rigorously to the day's stint of serious intellectual effort. Throughout his life he continued his college studies in French, German, science, history, philosophy, and theology. The textbooks in all six subjects were read to him as he sat and listened in the dark. When the morning's study was finished he began dictating the original work for which he soon became famous throughout the British Empire. His sermons, lectures, and magazine articles were prepared in this way, as well as the dozen books he published. Later in the day came the innumerable duties connected with parish visitation and church administration, and in the evening someone took him to the place where he completed the day's work by speaking in public. This was the blind man's daily schedule, a schedule which he followed without self-pity or self-distrust till he was past sixty. How simple our problem compared to his!

One day in 1882 Matheson happened to be entirely alone in the manse in Edinburgh. Something had happened which brought him what he called "the most severe mental suffering." To his great credit he never told other people, even the members of his own family, what it was. Sitting alone in that empty house, and recalling the long, dark years since his eyes had failed in boyhood, he began composing a poem. It has been used ever since as a hymn, and its words have become familiar to numberless Christians. To anyone who knows the story of Matheson's hard, discouraging life the most impressive thing about the poem is its utter freedom from the self-pity and fear which would have been only too natural under the circumstances.

> O Love that wilt not let me go
> I rest my weary soul in Thee;
> I give Thee back the life I owe
> That in Thine ocean depths its flow
>   May richer, fuller be.
>
> O Joy that seekest me through pain
> I cannot close my heart to Thee;
> I trace the rainbow through the rain
> And feel the promise is not vain
>   That morn shall tearless be.

If George Matheson could conquer self-fear you and I can conquer it too. If he could find a rainbow in his sky we can certainly locate one somewhere in ours.

CHAPTER VI

MANAGING PERSONAL RELATIONSHIPS

I

ONE of the most interesting characters in the Bible is the elder brother mentioned in the parable of the Prodigal Son.[1] What was the flaw in his personality? It was not, as in the case of the younger brother, sensuality. According to the story the elder son had always led an exemplary life. Neither was his weakness inefficiency as a worker. The parable implies that this older boy had served his father faithfully and well for many years. An upright and a hard-working person . . . yet he had one serious defect. In a crisis he could not get along with other people. In a difficult human situation he did exactly the wrong thing.

When the elder brother came in from the field and learned that his brother had unexpectedly re-

[1] Luke xv. 11-32.

turned he should, of course, have hurried into the house and—regardless of his own secret emotions—greeted the Prodigal affectionately. When he found that his father was overjoyed at the younger brother's return and that a feast was being prepared in honor of the event, he should have stifled his resentment and envy and joined enthusiastically in the celebration. A man who knew how to manage personal relationships would have done all these things. But the elder brother stayed angrily outside the house and refused to speak pleasantly to anyone. This of course made his father highly indignant, and earned for him the permanent enmity of his younger brother. However admirable this elder son may have been in some ways there was one point at which he failed lamentably. He could not deal with people. He could not manage human relationships.

The modern world is filled with individuals of this type. Their moral record may be beyond question, and in their work they may show steady and highly commendable efficiency. But in the field of personal contacts their record is pitiful. In a critical human situation they invariably antagonize someone. Some of these individuals can trace their difficulties, as the elder brother could, to the combination of sensitiveness and envy. If anyone in the vicinity attracts more attention or wins more praise than they do, they promptly take offense. If someone slights them or fails to show proper consideration for their feelings or their opinions, they invariably make a scene. Other people have difficulty in personal relationships because they give the impression of being self-centered and unsympathetic. At the times when their friends crave expressions of interest and appreciation these individuals invariably seem aloof or even hostile. Recently an English author published a volume bearing this strange dedication, "To my wife: whose lack of interest in this volume has been my constant despair." What a picture of a woman who had never learned to manage human contacts!

But perhaps the greatest source of difficulty in human relationships is the attitude of cocksureness. How annoyed we are when we meet some one who acts and talks as though he could tell us everything and we could tell him nothing!

How swiftly his "know-it-all" bearing rouses our antagonism! During the most crucial period in the Civil War, when Lee's troops were invading Pennsylvania, a cocksure civilian in Philadelphia telegraphed General Halleck in Washington offering his services as commander-in-chief of the Federal forces. He implied he could win the war in a week if he were only given the chance. General Halleck sent him this grim reply. "We already have five times as many Generals as we want, but we are greatly in need of private soldiers. Anyone volunteering in that capacity will be very welcome. What do yau say?" What a misfortune it would have been to live near that conceited Philadelphian! Had he really gone to the front his neighbors would have been overjoyed.

One of the things each of us owes the people about him is an occasional hour of rigid self-scrutiny on this point. How do we really impress our associates? Most of us assume, as we have always done, that the people about us consider us kind-hearted, thoughtful, and easy to work with. But what if that notion is frankly optimistic? Most of us fancy that the members of our own family love us as deeply and regard us as highly as they did ten years ago. But what if our gruff manners, our stony silences, and our occasional sallies of sarcasm have gradually aroused a bitter resentment? Facing one's self honestly and trying to gauge accurately one's success in handling people may not be a pleasant undertaking. But all of us ought to make the venture, at least occasionally. It is only through rigid self-examination that we can locate the unfortunate attitudes and the irritating mannerisms which wreck our friendships. It is only by heroic self-discipline that we can eliminate these defects from our personality.

II

When we attempt such a self-analysis there are several facts which, in fairness to ourselves, we ought to bear in mind. The most obvious is this. There is no possible way by which we can please everyone. No matter how wise, how kind, and how self-forgetful we are, there will always be at least a few people who will not be enthusiastic over us. Why? Partly because human tempera-

ments vary. The individuals who take little interest in moral and religious problems, and who are
not concerned over attempts to develop the intellectual and the spiritual life of a community,
invariably remain aloof from such people as
ministers, teachers, and reformers. No matter
how wise the ministers and teachers may be, and
no matter how deep the need for the work the
reformers are doing, the non-intellectual and non-
idealistic human types will invariably show indifference or even active hostility toward them. The
major responsibility for this conflict lies not with
the individuals involved. Rather it lies with life,
life which has made each one of us "indescribably
himself."

In other cases antipathy is traceable to jealousy.
When the average man meets a rival who has
persistently outclassed him the average man feels
toward that rival an immediate, bitter, and ineradicable dislike. What queer mannerisms he has!
How snobbish and self-satisfied he seems! How
plain it is that his success has spoiled him! So
the individual in second place reasons, little
dreaming that this alleged analysis of the other

man's character is merely jealousy in disguise. If you and I enjoy a measure of success, and if in the winning of that success we have superseded some one else, we can be reasonably sure that the person we have surpassed will develop a permanent dislike of us. When we scrutinize our record in managing people we must, in fairness to ourselves, remember these facts. We must not expect ourselves to win enthusiastic approval from everyone. Even Jesus never succeeded in doing that.

It is also well to realize that even within the small group of our devoted friends we cannot always win agreement and applause. Why? Because, even assuming that our opinions are well founded and our efforts highly commendable, our friends frequently have moods. They are not always in a condition to understand what we are saying or to appreciate what we are doing. Sometimes they are carrying heavy but secret burdens, sometimes they are the victims of fatigue, sometimes they are smarting under criticism or defeat. In such black moments they are likely to prove unsympathetic, unappreciative, and unresponsive. While their mood lasts we must not expect too much from them, and we certainly must not take too seriously the hasty and ill-considered remarks they make. One of our modern poets has recently drawn a remarkable picture of the situation we have been describing. She entitles her poem "Tired."

> No, do not ask me to be wise.
>   I have no thoughts at all.
> Only that life is swift, and flies
>   Shadow-like, strange, and small.
>
> Only that I am less than dew,
>   And frailer than a fern.
> I have forgotten all I knew
>   Of certainty. To learn
>
> This much is harder than I guessed.
>   I will not pass for wise.
> I am too tired for a quest,
>   Too sleepy for surmise.[2]

When our friends are in such a mood we must not expect to please them. The stage is set for indifference and irresponsible criticism on their part rather than for friendship, appreciation, and discerning judgment.

[2] From Fannie Stearns Davis Gifford, *The Ancient Beautiful Things*. By permission of The Macmillan Company, publishers.

There is still another fact all of us should recall. A man must not expect himself to equal the popularity record of the individuals who are more favorably situated for the task of winning and keeping friends. Consider this case. Two young men graduated from college the same year and married at the same time. One became a traveling salesman, and was assigned such a huge territory that he had to spend practically all his time on the road. He found a place near the center of his territory where his wife and children could live, and he paid them flying visits as often as he could. But the situation soon proved abnormal and unsatisfactory. The man himself could not win friendships anywhere, and his wife and children found it impossible to enter the social life of their community as they would have done had the family been united. The final result of the situation was an obvious isolation and a pitiful friendlessness for everyone.

Meantime the other young man and his family had had an entirely different experience. This second man studied law, entered politics, won an important election in the city of his boyhood, and then settled there permanently as one of the influential municipal officials. Thanks to his intimate acquaintance with the community and his important political position his home soon became the center of a network of social activities and happy personal relationships. For him and his family it proved a simple matter to win and keep friends, gain community-wide recognition and esteem. Does the sharp contrast between the final situation of the two classmates indicate that one is a failure in managing people while the other is a success? Nothing of the kind. All it indicates is that the first man has had far less than the normal chance to make friends, while the second man has had far more.

In the light of all these facts how much success can the average person hope for in the field of human relationships? How many friends can he fairly expect to win? All of us should brace ourselves for the discovery that we have at least a few enemies, and beyond them a host of acquaintances who care little or nothing about us and our affairs. But we can confidently expect, if we manage people in a reasonably intelligent and effective way, that we shall also have a circle of acquaintances who will be genuinely interested in us, and within that circle at least a few friends who will care deeply for us. The love we find in this final group may well enable us to overlook the indifference and hostility we encounter elsewhere. As a matter of fact the affection, loyalty, and understanding of one other individual may meet in full our need for friendship and devotion.

If I can bear your love like a lamp before me
When I go down the long, steep road of darkness,
I shall not fear the everlasting shadows
   Nor cry in terror.

If I can find God then I shall find Him,
If none can find Him then I shall sleep soundly;
Knowing how well on earth your love sufficed me—
   A lamp in darkness.[3]

III

How now can we increase our ability to manage personal relationships? What are the changes we can make in ourselves which will enable us to win more friends and hold more firmly those

[3] From Sara Teasdale, *Love Songs*. By permission of The Macmillan Company, publishers.

we already have? The conventional way in which to answer those questions is to enumerate a long list of familiar virtues—considerateness, patience, courtesy, and the like—and then urge their cultivation. Suppose, instead of following this obvious procedure, we study three human tendencies which must be guarded with special care if we are to make a success of our relationships with other people.

To begin with, all of us must control rigidly our desire to capture attention. Repeatedly it is this desire which brings us into difficulty with other people. Have you ever watched a group of kindergarten children talking with their teacher? The obvious desire of each child is to gain that teacher's exclusive attention. One youngster takes his stand directly in front of the teacher, points insistently at his new shoes, and explains at the top of his lungs that they were a birthday present. Another child tugs vigorously at the teacher's sleeve, and tries to concentrate her attention on the row of brass buttons on his overcoat. Still a third child elbows his way energetically past all his rivals, thrusts into the teacher's hands a picture he has just completed, and explains loudly that it is a better picture than any one else can draw. The thirst for attention, the passion for notice, the dread of being overlooked—how familiar this trait is in boys and girls!

Unhappily this trait persists with almost unmodified vigor in many older people. The expression of the instinct may be less frank and unashamed, but anyone who knows the mechanics of human conduct soon recognizes the childish impulse underlying the behavior of the adult. Here, for example, is a woman who dresses in extreme styles, cultivates a noisy manner, and at public meetings invariably makes her way to a seat near the platform and asks questions as soon as the meeting is thrown open for discussion. What is it she craves? Any kindergarten teacher can tell you. This woman wants to be noticed. The thought she may be overlooked is almost unendurable to her. Or here is a woman who makes it a practice to pass on to other people every unkind remark about them she happens to hear. If there is a dearth of such conversational material this woman devises caustic comments of her own, comments which invariably make the listener wince. It is the special delight of such a woman to tell a minister at the close of an exhausting service that his sermon did not quite come up to expectations, and to inform her physician with a wry smile that she thinks a change in medical advisers might possibly benefit her. What is the underlying motive in such strange actions? It is the desire to be noticed. This woman cannot attract an adequate amount of attention by creditable methods, and thus she reverts to cruel gibes and sarcastic comments. Even if people dislike her she will at least not be overlooked!

In this same category belong the individuals who, by one means or another, make constant bids for sympathy. What they really seek is not so much affection as notice. They cannot bear to think they have been forgotten, or feel they are crowded into an obscure corner of their friends' world. How often, for instance, we find a man sitting glumly at the dinner table, and then retiring to the living-room dragging what his high-school son terms "one of the great northern silences" after him. Everyone in the family becomes more and more conscious of his presence, and finally there are family-wide efforts to learn what ails Father and how his all-too-obvious distress can be relieved. One of the children brings the evening paper, and another fetches Father's slippers. Someone else attempts a funny story, and then Mother dashes to the telephone to prevent the advent of disastrous news from the outside world. As the resources of the entire household are thus mobilized to restore Father's cheerfulness, and as every member of the family works harder and harder to understand Father's feelings and anticipate his desires, Father brightens perceptibly and finally begins to conduct himself in normal fashion. What is the secret of his strange actions? Father has reverted to the child level and made a desperate bid for attention. Now that he is obviously noticed, noticed by everyone in the family, he is as happy as the youngster who has finally monopolized the attention of the kindergarten teacher.

Those of us who are in earnest about increasing our ability to get along with other people should watch ourselves with the utmost care at this point.

The individual who dresses conspicuously and courts publicity inevitably rouses antagonism. The person who captures attention by criticizing everything and everybody soon makes a host of enemies. The individual who appeals for sympathy whenever there is even one friend or relative in the vicinity soon finds himself cordially disliked. Repeatedly it is an awkward attempt to capture attention which is responsible for difficulties in human relationships. Repeatedly it is the determination to conquer this childish impulse which marks the beginning of new achievements in friendship.

Another childish impulse all of us must guard is the impulse to make other people unhappy whenever we ourselves are unhappy. How clearly this instinct appears in little children! When youngsters are hurt, either physically or emotionally, they want other people to be hurt too. Those other people must give, somehow, evidences of great discomfort and extreme solicitude. If those other people are indifferent, or make the mistake of taking the matter in hand lightly, the child's pain instantly becomes more acute. How does

anyone dare laugh when this youngster himself
is crying? Many adults, as we all realize, carry
this childish tendency into the world of maturity.
When things go wrong these adults start immediate efforts to make some one else miserable too.
Sometimes they achieve this end by bullying the
chauffeur or criticizing outrageously the efforts
of an apprehensive and timorous stenographer.
Sometimes they assuage their own pain by piling
new and heavy burdens on their subordinates or
on the general public. Sometimes they yield to a
vicious cruelty impulse and deliberately hurt the
very person they love best.

During the World War an American officer
stationed on the French front was assigned the
task of censoring all the letters which were mailed
in his section. In an article published in the
Atlantic Monthly after the Armistice he recounted
some of his experiences. During the course of
the article he made this discerning comment on
human nature. "I wonder why it is we deliberately hurt the very people we love best. I suppose
it is because we are still children at heart, and
because like children we want to see some one

else cry too. One day an officer came quietly to our mail-box and, when he thought no one was looking, hastily abstracted a letter he had written to his wife and tore it up. I knew why he destroyed that cruel missive. I had read the letter myself." As long as such childish impulses dominate our lives we cannot expect people to love us. How can they continue to feel affection and sympathy if, when we ourselves are wounded, we instantly seek to inflict pain on them?

There is still a third tendency which all of us must guard with scrupulous care. It is the childish tendency to give others only as much as we get from them, and to try to take from others exactly as much as we have previously given them. This calculating impulse appears clearly in all youngsters. What vigorous expressions of it we detect in the conversations overheard from the nursery! "Why should I let him take my scooter? He wouldn't let me take his." "Why should I invite her to my party? She didn't invite me to hers." Here is the calculating spirit in its clearest, least concealed form. Curiously enough, the remarks of many older people disclose this same spirit. "Why should I give my money to the poor? The poor have never done anything for me." "Why should I keep on helping and forgiving other people? They show no evidence of returning my kindness." The result of this spirit, in the life of children and in the life of adults, is pitifully familiar. It leads swiftly and inevitably to the destruction of friendship, and the progressive isolation of the selfish, calculating individual who is dominated by it.

Here and there we find men and women who, like Jesus, completely conquer this impulse toward persistent self-consideration. These individuals are ready to show kindness no matter how little kindness comes to them in return, they are ready to forgive even if their friendliness wakens no apparent response, and they are ready to share no matter how few and inadequate the exhibitions of sharing on the part of those who benefit by their generosity. When such an individual appears in a community he makes, as Jesus made, an indelible impression. Emerson stated the truth in one of his characteristic epigrams. "See how the mass of men worry themselves into nameless graves, while here and there a few unselfish souls forget themselves into immortality!" Such unselfish people have discovered the ultimate secret of managing human relationships. They have learned that love, self-forgetful and unfaltering love, is the strongest power in life.

Some months ago the city missionary in a New England industrial center [4] died after an illness of only a few hours. Her death evoked innumerable expressions of admiration and devotion. Perhaps the most striking tribute came from a twelve-year-old Greek girl whose family had been assisted on numberless occasions by this self-forgetful, Christlike woman. This child wrote, "When we first came to Springfield my father could not support our family. While he was looking for work a friend told him about Mrs. Mallary and brought her to our house. She attends to any call, whether it is to sick, poor, or funerals. All the days of the week she goes to the hospital to see the foreign people there. When I was in the hospital she came to see me. The days after I was operated on when I opened my eyes there

[4] Mrs. Lucy W. Mallary of Springfield, Massachusetts.

was Mother Mallary. Every day she came she brought for me sometimes flowers, books, fruit, and company. The night before Christmas a big box came to our house by express. My mother was astonished and did not know what to do. But when my father came home he opened it boldly, and there were dolls, games, ribbons, and also a rattle for our new baby. This is the reason Mother Mallary is loved by everybody. All the Greek people try their best to thank her. As long as I live I will never forget her." Why did that woman have literally a host of friends? Because she had forgotten herself completely. Because all she asked was how much she could do for others.

CHAPTER VII

KEEPING ENTHUSIASTIC ABOUT ONE'S JOB

I

SOME time ago a school-teacher sent me this unusual letter. "I wonder if you could help me with one of my personal problems. I have been teaching for a number of years, and long ago all the newness wore off my work. Like most teachers in the thirties I have now settled down to a regular and a painfully familiar routine. My difficulty is that I often find myself beset by an almost uncontrollable restlessness and dissatisfaction. Some days it seems as if I couldn't continue teaching another minute. When that mood passes it is followed by a mood of complete indifference toward my job. I lose all my interest in teaching. I realize that such feelings will be detrimental to the quality of my work, and I have tried repeatedly to conquer them. But in spite of all my efforts they keep coming. If you could tell me how to master these moods of restlessness, and maintain a steady interest in my school work, I should certainly appreciate it." What was the problem which this teacher was facing and which she here described so vividly? One of the most common in the world. The problem of keeping enthusiastic about one's job.

Most of us meet this problem by the time we are thirty if we have not met it before. It makes no difference what our job is, where it is located, or how successful we have been in it. A day finally comes when our work loses its original novelty and interest, and the long struggle to maintain our morale begins. It is an open secret that most ministers meet this situation after they have remained in a parish for five, or at the most, ten years. During the first year or two work in that church proved stimulating and satisfying because it brought a steady succession of new problems and fresh opportunities. There were new families to meet, new undertakings to plan, and new ideas to present to an attentive and an expectant congregation. The preacher's old sermons were suddenly new again, and no one in the congregation had heard even once his favorite illustrations or his original and highly ingenious texts. What a joy to preach under those circumstances! But after a few years the situation began to change. The minister knew all his people, and they knew him—possibly too well. He completed the process of reorganizing the church, and the limits of its expansion were definitely reached. The ideas in the preacher's mind became thoroughly familiar to everyone in the congregation, and the local skeptics who once showed signs of abandoning golf and attending church regularly were seen once more at the Country Club on Sunday mornings. Then what happened? Suddenly the minister concluded that work in that church was dull and unrewarding, and that his gifts fitted him admirably for work in a parish of an entirely different type—preferably at a great distance. It is reported that in 1930 no less than seventy-five per cent of the ministers in one of the largest Protestant denominations in the United States applied to denominational headquarters for a change in pastorate. Keeping enthusiastic about an old job—that was the problem all these restless men were facing.

The same problem crops up, of course, in every other field of work. President Eliot of Harvard once confessed, many years after he had assumed his position as head of the University, that his job no longer offered him either novelty or fresh interest. He went so far as to say that nine-tenths of it had become sheer routine, as dull and monotonous to him as the work of carpenters and blacksmiths is to them. We might imagine that the chief executive of a great university—facing tasks as varied as planning a curriculum, engaging and removing professors, raising funds, and erecting buildings—would find his work always new and always invigorating. But this is, apparently, not the case. It would be interesting to interview the men in other important executive positions—in the business, the industrial, the scientific, and the political world—and find how many of them are plagued by secret restlessness. The likelihood is that all of them have days when they would like nothing better than to resign from their present position and try some other career.

But it is in another field—in the field of domestic life and parental responsibilities—that this problem assumes its most acute and dangerous form. How many young married people wish secretly that they could run away from their present home and start again somewhere else! During the first weeks and months of marriage these difficulties seldom arise. The bride and groom find it relatively easy to make the personal adjustments which their new situation requires, and meet with a smile the demands for self-sacrifice which the half-furnished and half-organized home lays upon them. Both of them are still fascinated by the venture of living together, and they are still keenly interested in the home they have agreed to create. Even if it is measured by one room, a kitchenette, and a breakfast alcove it seems to them a corner—though admittedly a small corner —of Paradise. But as the years pass and the children come the situation gradually changes. The wedding silver grows dull and its pattern becomes hopelessly out of date. Home-making brings burdens and responsibilities which the bride and groom never expected, and the children force on the parents annoying restrictions and obligations which neither parent contemplated in the carefree days before the wedding. How often, as this new situation gradually takes shape, love gives place to indifference and loyalty to restlessness! How hard many young couples find it to maintain their enthusiasm for a task assumed light-heartedly ten years before!

One of our humorists recently drew an amusing picture of two young parents who were suddenly brought face to face with this problem. The wife wanted to spend Saturday afternoon shopping, and her husband—a statistician by profession—finally agreed under protest to abandon a prospective golf match and spend the afternoon guarding three small and energetic youngsters. When, a few hours later, the mother returned from her errands she heard sounds of unmistakable distress emerging from the house. As she opened the front door her husband handed her defiantly the list of things the children had asked him to do, together with the number of times each demand had been made. Here is his record, thrust angrily into the hands of "the children's mother."

Dried the children's tears 14 times
Tied their shoes 16 times
Served drinks of water 22 times
Toy balloons purchased—3 per child
Average life of a balloon—12 seconds
Cautioned children not to cross the street 34 times
Children insisted on crossing the street 34 times
Number of Saturdays father will do this in the
       future—NONE.

Not easy to keep enthusiastic about that job!

II

Suppose this problem, in one of its many forms, is confronting you. How can you solve it? How can you maintain your interest in the work you are now doing, your faith in its ultimate possibilities?

Before we try to answer those questions there are two points which should be stated clearly. The first is that many of our moods of discouragement and restlessness are temporary and trivial things, the by-products of fatigue. One of the ways in which physical or nervous exhaustion most frequently discloses itself is in a sudden feeling that our work amounts to nothing, that no one is interested in having us do it well, that our past record has been one of dismal failure, and that we cannot continue carrying our responsibilities a day longer. When a man finds such ideas creeping into his mind, when the normal radiance begins to fade from his tiny world, he can safely conclude that he is more tired than he realizes. As a result of this fatigue his perspective on himself and his work is temporarily distorted, and his verdict on his achievements is temporarily unreliable. One of the first and most important lessons all of us must learn is this lesson of self-knowledge. We must, by careful and persistent self-scrutiny, gain the ability to recognize our own symptoms of exhaustion, and win a thorough understanding of the methods by which our normal resilience and equilibrium can be restored. In one of his letters Martin Luther reveals the efforts he made in this direction, and the wisdom about himself and his moods which he finally won. A friend had written asking how to master the feeling of discouragement, and Luther sent this bluff reply. "Whenever the Devil vexes you with such thoughts immediately seek the society of men, or drink more freely, or talk nonsense, or do some hilarious thing. Why do you think I eat so often, drink so much, and converse with such freedom if not to make sport of the Devil when he is trying to vex and make sport of me?"[1] Luther's notion that there is a Devil who is responsible for our moods of despair faded long ago. Luther's pre-prohibition recipe for courage is now illegal, at least in the United States. But Luther's words show a knowledge of life which many of us might well envy. Many of our moods of restlessness and dissatisfaction have an insignificant origin. We can conquer them by the simple expedient of giving ourselves something to eat, putting ourselves to bed, and making ourselves stop talking.

The other preliminary fact we mention is equally obvious. There are many people in our world who ought not to content themselves with their present position and their present achievement. They ought to break free from the cramping restrictions of their little world, and find a new career which will give them the scope and the incentive they need. To suggest that everyone stay where he now is and try to make himself happy

[1] See A. C. McGiffert, *Martin Luther,* p. 300.

there would be to stifle the worthy ambition which is of such priceless value to our race. To imply that everyone can, if he will try hard enough, find satisfaction in his present career is to make an obvious denial of the facts.

Some fifty years ago a boy named Aaron Drucker was born in a village in the interior of Russia. His parents were desperately poor, the members of the family were often on the verge of starvation, and at the age of twelve Aaron started to walk to America. He had little idea where America was or how he could get there, but he had heard its glories from a traveler who claimed to have authentic information. After many adventures he reached Odessa and took ship to Constantinople. There some Russian officials discovered him and promptly sent him back to his own land. Undiscouraged by this failure Aaron bent his steps farther southward, crossed the Russo-German frontier, and eventually reached the city of Memel. There he located a job, saved every pfennig he could, and finally accumulated enough money to buy a passage to New York. In October 1891 he landed there—knowing only a few words of English, and boasting little cash and still fewer friends. His first job was packing shirts in a sweatshop on the East Side. Eventually he advanced and became a worker in a shirt factory. That was as far as he had progressed on his twenty-fifth birthday. That year a sudden ambition flamed within him, and he determined to learn English. He began as a kindergarten pupil in a noon-hour class organized for the immigrant workers in his factory. There he mastered the letters of the English alphabet, and then he turned eagerly to night school. At night school he prepared for Columbia University, and after his graduation from Columbia went to the University of Chicago for further study. Finally he won an appointment as Dean of the Commercial Department of Colorado College. At twenty-five he had been a pupil in a kindergarten, at fifty he was a college professor with degrees from both Columbia and the University of Chicago.[2] How fortunate that Aaron Drucker did not attempt to satisfy himself with his boyhood life in Russia or with his later life in an East Side sweatshop! There are

[2] See Archer Wallace, *Overcoming Handicaps,* pp. 119-126.

thousands of people to-day, particularly young people, who should emulate his example and strive to acquire at least some of his daring ambition and courage. To advise them to stay where they now are and content themselves with what they now have would be the worst sort of nonsense.

But when we have counseled ambition and courage there is something else to be said. There are thousands of people, most of them older people, who need attitudes and virtues of an entirely different type. These men and women cannot change their job, or alter materially the situation within which they now live and work. They must stay where they are, stay there because no honorable road of escape lies open. If you study the people in your acquaintance who are over thirty years of age you will be surprised to find how many of them belong in this group. When all is said, it is dubious wisdom for a school teacher who has gained professional training and years of actual teaching experience to scrap that equipment and attempt, late in the thirties, an entirely new line of work. It is doubtful whether the ministers and the business executives who have invested the years of youth and early maturity in the acquisition of certain skills and personal contacts should, in the thirties or forties, abandon their original plans and undertake a wholly new career. Swapping horses in midstream is not half so risky as swapping jobs in middle life. Certainly two young people who once uttered the solemn words, "Till death us do part," make a highly questionable decision when they suddenly conclude their home can never be happy and go their separate ways, leaving their bewildered children to pay the heavy price of the parents' failure in forbearance and sustained self-sacrifice. For every person who can make his way out of a difficult and disheartening job and locate a happier one, there are a dozen persons who cannot solve the problem of restlessness in this simple fashion. These persons must stay where they are, and by readjusting their own attitudes and expectations find the happiness they crave. They must solve the problem of an unsatisfactory environment not by leaving it but by adapting themselves more skillfully to it.

Suppose, when all is said, this is your task. Suppose there is no honorable road of escape from the world in which you now live and from the work you now find yourself doing. How can you make yourself happy where you are? How can you keep yourself enthusiastic about your present job?

III

Many of us, facing this difficulty, have found great help in locating and accepting the characteristic limitations of our career. If you study modern life carefully you will soon discover that every career has its own peculiar restrictions, every job its own characteristic difficulties. Consider the situation in the medical profession. Under normal circumstances a young physician works at least ten years after graduation from medical school before he succeeds in building up a good practice. During that period, and throughout his years of active service, he must hold himself at the beck and call of the public both day and night. He must also, in most instances, wait a bewilderingly long time for the money his patients owe him. The doctor's career an easy one? No one but the doctor and the doctor's wife knows how many drawbacks it has! Or consider the limitations in a business career. The business man may succeed in dodging the difficulties which a doctor meets, and in the course of his lifetime he may succeed in accumulating far more wealth than the doctor can acquire. Yet the business man invariably encounters problems and hardships of his own. To begin with, he soon learns that periods of prosperity are interrupted by periods of highly disconcerting depression. He cannot make money every year, and much of the time he must resign himself to the discouraging job of operating his business at an actual loss. He also discovers that competition, in every line of business, grows keener every year, and that unless he spurs himself to improve his goods and his services constantly some more efficient rival will take his customers away from him. Most disconcerting of all is the element of risk which attends every business venture. Investments may go wrong, a promising undertaking may be wrecked by the blunders or the dishonesty of a subordinate, and an entire industry may be swept away by a sudden and an unpredictable change in public taste. The business man's career easy? No one but the business man and his wife knows how many difficulties and anxieties attend it! What is true of these two careers is equally true of every career. Not one of them is wholly satisfactory. Each has its characteristic limitations, its essential and ineradicable drawbacks.

Why is it important for us to remember this fact? Because, if we do remember it, the difficulties connected with our own job gradually lose their power to bewilder and terrify us. If a man wants to be happy in his work, particularly if he must remain in it against his will, his first step toward satisfaction and contentment is to locate the limitations inherent in his career, accept them with a smile, and then refuse to let himself be annoyed or disheartened by them. Their presence in his life is no indication that he is either inefficient or out of place. His constant struggle against them is no unfair burden piled on him by malicious circumstance. If he left his present job and attempted another he would discover there hardships which, though different in type, would be equally severe. Therefore he can make up his mind to stay where he is, and stay there without bitterness or despair. His burdens are no heavier than those of other men.

The next step away from restlessness and toward contentment is to recognize the fact that one's job, whatever it is, has peculiar advantages as well as peculiar limitations. It brings problems of its own but also satisfactions of its own. The tendency of most people, particularly at the times when they are overtired, is to become acutely conscious of the characteristic hardships of their career and entirely oblivious of its characteristic opportunities and advantages. A traveling salesman, disheartened by his unimpressive record during a period of protracted business depression, tells himself bitterly that selling is the worst job imaginable. He forgets that a traveling salesman has at least two distinct advantages over the man who is employed during stated hours in a stated place. The traveling salesman is master of his own time and his own movements. He also has an unusual chance to develop originality and then gain full and undisputed credit for it. A trained nurse, exhausted by the ceaseless demands of a fretty patient, comes to her minister in tears to say she bitterly regrets her choice of a profession, and to inquire whether the minister knows any business position which she might secure. The minister must quietly remind the nurse that her job has special advantages as well as the special limitations of which she is, for the moment, so acutely conscious. The nurse's career offers her the chance to help individuals through their most desperate hours of need, and in the process win friendships and gain a type of gratitude which the average business woman never knows. Two young parents, bewildered by the unexpected personal and financial demands made upon them by their children, suddenly conclude that home-making and child-training are essentially impossible tasks, and that they themselves would be far happier if they had never attempted the ventures of marriage and parenthood at all. But in their wiser and quieter moments these same young people realize, as numberless parents have realized before them, that a home and children are worth far more than they cost, and that our world is filled with childless men and women who would give literally all they possess for the love and the happiness which children, and nothing else, would bring.

Why does it help us thus to focus our attention on the favorable elements in our own situation? Partly because this action gives us confidence that our work can bring us the satisfaction we crave, and partly because this action frees us from a peculiarly dangerous type of jealousy—jealousy of the people who are in a job different from ours. When we force ourselves to recall and contemplate the peculiar advantages of the career we are following, advantages we should instantly lose if we shifted to an alternative career, we gain an entirely new attitude toward our own life. We gradually awake to the fact that other people undoubtedly envy us quite as bitterly as we envy them. When that truth dawns on the mind the victory over restlessness is near at hand.

Quite as helpful is the practice of picturing one's job in high terms rather than low ones. One day, at the reunion of a class which had graduated from college twenty years before, a stockbroker who had accumulated an immense fortune

approached a classmate who had spent the years
since graduation teaching in a preparatory school.
The stockbroker, who had a fine scorn of non-
financial achievements, said with half-concealed
sarcasm, "So you teach Greek!" There was a
moment of embarrassed silence, and then the
teacher answered quietly, "No, you're wrong. I
teach boys. Greek is what I start with." Those
words suggest the right and the wrong way of
interpreting any career. We may count the work
involved as a narrow cage within which a rebellious human spirit paces wearily, always seeking a
way of escape to some broader world. Or we may
regard the same task as a doorway through which
a creative personality goes out day after day to
serve and bless other people. What one man calls
the dull job of discussing Homer another, and a
far more discerning, man recognizes is the superb
responsibility of training the men of the future.

In some careers, notably teaching, medicine,
and social service, these adjacent fields of opportunity are obvious. Are these similar possibilities
on other lines of work? If we translate these
other jobs into human terms, looking behind the

articles that are being manufactured and the services which are being rendered to the human beings who are being served, we soon realize that every worthy career has its wider and its immensely significant implications. Many business men give themselves a new pride in their work and a new confidence in its social value by thinking of their job, not as the task of stealing a few pennies of profit from unsuspecting customers, but as the task of providing the community with something it must have, and doing this work with a maximum of skill and at a minimum of expense. Many employers have won a new enthusiasm for their undertaking and a new pride in their accomplishment by regarding their factory, not as a place where an individual owner amasses a private fortune, but as a place where regular work at good wages is provided for hundreds of men who must find a job or starve. A similar reinterpretation of the daily task is the thing which has enabled the men and women who work with defectives to continue patiently their peculiarly difficult efforts. A century ago a kind-hearted doctor in Boston assumed the responsibility of trying to help a forlorn little girl who had been born blind, deaf, and dumb. There seemed no way by which that imprisoned personality could be reached, no way by which the eager doctor could transmit even the beginnings of knowledge to that silent, sightless, unresponsive child. But listen to Dr. Howe's own account of his efforts with Laura Bridgman. See in what high, brave terms he pictured his undertaking. "It was just like fishing. A man baits his hook, lets down his line, and then sits and waits for half an hour. Nothing happens. Then he pulls up the line, puts on a different bait, and tries again. For days and weeks I kept letting my line down to Laura. For six months there was no sign of response. Then one day while I was dangling a new bait I felt a sudden tug. I pulled up the line, and Laura's soul came up into the light." [8] A tiresome, meaningless job? Not when Dr. Howe interpreted it as the capture of a soul.

Here is a final suggestion. In our moments of restlessness let us recall the fact that other people have entrusted us with our work, and that they

[8] See *Religion in the Colleges* (Association Press, 1928), p. 39.

are relying on us to do it faithfully and well. Repeatedly it is the thought of the confidence other people have in us, the realization that our friends are expecting us to measure up to their high expectations, which sends us back to our task ready and willing to try again. Did you ever compute the number of people who have a stake in your faithfulness, your allegiance to duty? Consider the case of a young man employed in a bank. Around him stand literally thousands of men, women, and children whose lives are measurably affected by the way in which he does his work. To begin with, the officials of the bank have given him their building, their equipment, their reputation for reliability, and the clientele they have built up by years of painstaking effort. If that young man goes wrong, or if he merely proves ineffective, they and their institution will be seriously damaged. Beyond that immediate group is the wider circle of the young man's family and friends. They have given him their affection and their confidence, and they expect him to render a good account of himself even if his job does have many dull moments and a few serious drawbacks. If that young man proves dishonest those friends will be smirched by his disgrace, and that young man's children will be known to the end of their days as the sons and daughters of a thief. Beyond this second circle is a still wider circle which covers the entire nation. It is made up of banking men everywhere, men whose work rests on the foundation of public trust and confidence. When anyone in their group, even a man who occupies a subordinate position, proves recreant to a trust, the colossal task of maintaining public confidence becomes even more difficult than it was before. Thoughtless observers may claim that what this young man does with his own life is his own affair, but a careful study of the entire situation discloses their appalling mistake. What this young man does with his own life is the affair of literally thousands of other people. He must measure up to their expectations. He must be faithful to his job, no matter what rebellious thoughts surge through his mind and what discouragement rises within his heart.

On one of the reefs in New York harbor stands

a lighthouse which for many years was tended by
a widow—Mrs. Katie Walker. One day she told
her story to a reporter on a New York paper, and
he gave it to the world. She said, "I was living at
Sandy Hook when I first met my husband. He
took me to that lighthouse as his bride. I enjoyed
the life there, for the light was on land and we
could have a garden and raise flowers. But one
day the Government transferred us to this light
on Robbins Reef, surrounded by water. The day
we came I said to him, 'I can't stay here. The sight
of water wherever I look makes me too lonesome.'
I refused to unpack my trunks and boxes, but
somehow they seemed to get unpacked, and I've
been here ever since. It's almost forty years. One
night my husband caught a heavy cold while tending the light. It turned into pneumonia, and they
took him to the Infirmary on Staten Island while
I stayed here to watch the light in his place. A
few nights later, as I was sitting there tending the
lamp, I saw a boat coming. Something told me
the news it was bringing, and I expected to hear
the words that came up out of the dark. 'We're
sorry, but your husband's worse.' 'You mean he's

dead,' I answered, and they made no reply. We buried him on the mainland over there. Every morning when the sun comes up I stand at this porthole and look toward his grave. Sometimes the hills are brown, sometimes they are green, sometimes they are white with snow. But they always bring a message from him. Something I heard him say more often than anything else. Just three words—'Mind the light!' "

Who could disappoint a trust like that?

CHAPTER VIII

WATCHING THE OTHER PERSON WIN

I

ONE of the less familiar passages in the Book of Acts tells how the early Christians chose a successor to Judas.[1] There was a natural desire that a man of better type be appointed to fill the vacant place, and two candidates were nominated. Instead of determining their relative merits by investigation and discussion as we should do, Peter and his companions made the choice by offering prayer and then drawing lots. The early Christians shared the common belief of antiquity that in such a situation God could be trusted to manipulate the lots in such a way that the right man would be chosen. The lots were drawn, a man named Matthias was selected, and his rival— a man named Justus—was left to console himself as best he could. Imagine Justus' feelings as he

[1] Acts i. 15-26.

subsequently reviewed the events of that disappointing day. Imagine his feelings as, for years afterwards, he watched Matthias filling a position of honor and importance which had almost been his. Life could not have been easy for Justus. He had to face one of the hardest tests human nature knows—the test of seeing the other person win.

Sooner or later all of us meet this test. In different lives it assumes different forms, but in one guise or another it eventually comes to everyone. No matter how successful we may be in certain fields or at certain times, we eventually discover other fields or other situations in which we are hopelessly outclassed. There, gracefully or bitterly, we must watch a rival capture the honors.

Consider the situation which almost invariably emerges in a home in which there are several children. One of the youngsters proves to have gifts far greater than those of his brothers and sisters. Year by year he wins honors and gains distinctions which are utterly beyond their reach. Not an easy situation for the less gifted children! Or think of this difficulty as it develops in the business world.

The president of a large corporation dies, and each of the three vice presidents promptly assumes that the directors will award him the coveted position. But to the astonishment and chagrin of all three the directors announce they have offered the vacant position to a man from outside, a man who —so it is explained—will "bring new blood" into the company. The day comes when the three disappointed candidates must meet their superior. An easy moment as those men are ushered into the new president's office? If you think so, you know little about human nature.

But it is in another field that the most difficult form of this test emerges. Our world is filled with men and women who are compelled to watch other people enjoying the romance, the home, and the children they themselves hoped to have. They see these other parents living in an earthly paradise, they turn and contemplate their own bare and dismal world, and then a flood of bitterness sweeps over them. Why do they have so little when other people have so much? Why has their marriage been a failure when in these other cases marriage has been such a success? Watching the other person win . . . how familiar the problem, how difficult the test!

Many people, meeting this problem, prove wholly unable to solve it. However well they acquit themselves as winners they make a pitiful showing as losers. Certain individuals, for example, develop a furious jealousy when they find themselves outclassed. Sometimes this jealousy discloses itself as an irrational and enduring hatred of their rival. Sometimes it appears as the habit of criticizing bitterly and unfairly everything he says and does. Sometimes it takes the form of a churlish manner whenever that rival enters the room. The political world offers thousands of examples of this inability to accept defeat. So, unfortunately, does the professional world. The jealousy between doctors, musicians, and (worst of all) ministers, has now become proverbial. How hard it is to find, in any of these fields, an individual who will say a good word about the man who has persistently outclassed him!

Meantime other people, meeting an unexpected defeat, take an entirely different course. They develop a fatal feeling of self-distrust, a tragic

inferiority complex. In spite of the repeated
efforts their friends make to encourage them, and
in spite of the fine record they themselves made
until the day of the great disappointment, these
men and women never succeed in outgrowing the
effects of their major defeat. To the day of their
death they think of themselves as incompetents
and speak of themselves as second-raters. As they
begin each new venture they tell themselves that
luck will undoubtedly turn against them, and that
there is not one chance in ten this new undertaking will prove successful. The results of this attitude are, of course, disastrous. These individuals
find themselves unable to generate a normal
amount of self-confidence, courage, and power to
achieve. They find themselves persistently beaten,
and by a curiously illogical reasoning they attrib-
ute these reiterated defeats to a permanent incompetence rather than to the habit of self-distrust
which grew out of their inability to accept an
initial disappointment gracefully.

But worst of all are the men and women who,
forced to endure an unexpected defeat, vent their
spleen on innocent bystanders, particularly the

members of their own family. How familiar this human type is! One is tempted to speculate about events in Justus' home when Justus, after the disastrous competition with Matthias, returned to his wife and children. Did he show a commendable self-control and considerateness, or did he bring a thunder storm into the house with him? Was he as genial and good-natured as usual, or did he slump into such a prolonged and morose silence that the members of the family wished he had never been nominated at all? It is not enough merely to accept defeat. All of us must learn to accept it in good spirit. We must learn to watch the other person win, and then rigorously refrain from following the familiar impulse to make some one else share our misery.

One of the promising developments in modern education is the new effort now being made to teach children this quality of good sportsmanship. If you study modern homes and modern schools you will be surprised to find how many people are working early and late to make boys and girls good losers as well as good winners. Numberless parents, for example, are making every effort to teach their children to rejoice in one another's successes, and regard any triumph won by any member of the family as a family rather than an individual achievement. How much better this training than the training which rouses each child to an intense and lifelong competition with his brothers and sisters! Similarly in many schools there are ingenious and persistent efforts to teach all the youngsters to take victory without undue elation and (more important still) to accept defeat without bitterness. No one can estimate the value of this acquired ability in the inevitable crises of later years. In the better summer camps, to which thousands of children are now sent year by year, the effort to teach good sportsmanship reaches its climax. Every youngster in the camp is compelled to take part in competitive games and ingeniously arranged contests, and the child who whimpers, sulks, or makes himself disagreeable after a defeat is instantly dubbed a "poor loser" and condemned by everyone. After a few weeks of such discipline children begin to gain one of the most valuable traits of character we know— the ability to watch the other person win, and do so without evidences of inward distress or outward resentment.

The result of this modern training is that the better young people of to-day now reveal a quality of character which their elders might well envy. Consider the account of the famous tennis match between William Tilden and William Johnston at the Germantown Cricket Club in 1922. The national singles title was at stake, and also the permanent possession of a huge trophy which each man had won twice. Johnston was at a distinct disadvantage in both height and reach, but by an astonishing exhibition of skill and pluck he won the first two of the five sets. Tilden won the third, and then after the rest period Johnston captured the first three games of the crucial fourth set. Only three more games to win, and then the title and the trophy would be his! But during the next game the tide turned against Johnston, and Tilden—utilizing to the full his advantage in height and reach—eventually ran out the set and the match. What took place between the two men afterwards Tilden disclosed in a newspaper article. He wrote, "Johnston met me in the locker-

house, and congratulated me in all sincerity. I
shall always remember what he said in that
moment of disappointment. It was the most
sportsmanlike thing imaginable. 'Bill, I played
the best tennis of my life; but it just wasn't as
good as yours.' In all the years I have played
Johnston, sometimes beating him and sometimes
having him beat me, I have never seen him display any undue elation over a victory, or heard
him offer any alibi in defeat." What higher com-
pliment could one man pay another?

II

How can you and I gain this spirit? How can
we enlarge our ability to manage disappointment
and defeat? We might well begin our effort by
recalling the fact that every failure, no matter
how galling, may be used constructively. We can,
if we will, learn something of priceless value
from the experience of being beaten.

Obviously our defeats give us the chance to
show good sportsmanship, and by doing so gain
the admiration of those who are watching. If you
study crowds carefully you will soon discover that,

at the end of any contest, people are quite as much interested in the deportment of the loser as in that of the winner. How will the loser take his defeat? Will he knock the tennis balls over the grandstand, stare angrily at the referee, mumble incoherent sentences about unfair decisions, and then stalk angrily off the court? Or will he run to the net to congratulate his rival, walk to the locker house smiling, admit in his newspaper article the next day that he was outplayed, and then enroll in the next tournament and play harder than ever? The crowd waits to see. The moment of defeat brings any loser a golden opportunity. If he summons his self-control and takes his disappointment in the right spirit, he can win in that instant a host of admirers whom he never could have won in any other way.

Thousands of better-than-average people have proved this true. Every city has its story of the political candidate who lost the election, but who then acted so like a gentleman that he emerged from the experience of being beaten with greater popular esteem than ever. Every business house can tell of a man who was not promoted as he

expected, but who accepted his defeat gracefully
and proceeded to work so faithfully and so well
that he finally made himself indispensable to the
concern. Many churches still point with pride to
an elderly minister who, succeeded by a younger
man, steadily refused to criticize his successor's
mistakes, and finally made himself beloved by
everyone in the community—the new preacher
included. All these individuals prove to the rest
of us that a man who possesses adequate self-control can transform his hour of defeat into an hour
of significant victory.

Quite as evident is the fact that our defeats
will, if we use them in the right way, give us
priceless information about ourselves. We can
gain from those defeats, as from nothing else, an
accurate perspective on our methods of working,
and a knowledge of the points at which our technique should be improved. In the short autobiography which Charles Darwin wrote for his children we find this significant statement. "I have
also, during many years, followed a golden rule
—whenever a published fact, a new observation,
or a thought which is opposed to my general

results comes to me, to make a memorandum of it without fail and at once. For I have found by experience that such facts and thoughts are far more apt to escape from my memory than favorable ones." [2] What a picture of a man who was learning from defeat, gaining wisdom from the facts which contradicted his own theories! There is a painful contrast between the attitude which Darwin revealed and the hot-tempered and unteachable spirit which Martin Luther disclosed in a similar situation. To one of his critics Luther wrote angrily, "Never have I seen a more ignorant ass than you are, though you particularly boast of having studied dialectics. I greatly rejoice at being condemned by so obscure a head!" [3] With such an attitude Luther was not likely to learn wisdom from this critic, or gain new knowledge from the objections this man raised against his teaching. Darwin, laboriously collecting all the negative evidence, was certain to profit from his critics as well as from his admirers, from his defeats as well as from his victories. Numberless people

[2] See H. E. Fosdick, *Adventurous Religion*, p. 115.
[3] See A. C. McGiffert, *Martin Luther*, p. 151.

to-day, cultivating Darwin's attitude rather than Luther's, have located their mistakes, discovered their shortcomings, corrected their blunders, and eventually raised themselves to a new and a higher level of achievement. They have employed criticism, disappointment, and defeat not merely as means of winning admiration from those who were watching, but also as means of gaining information about themselves—information of priceless value to one who has enough open-mindedness, composure, and intelligence to make use of it.

III

We can also remind ourselves, whenever we are compelled to watch the other person win, that the loser in a struggle may possibly be quite as able and deserving a person as the winner. The victor's triumph may demonstrate that he is the , better man of the two, and then again it may demonstrate nothing of the sort. Why this element of uncertainty? Because coincidence plays an enormous part in human affairs. Repeatedly it is good fortune which brings one man success, and bad fortune which brings his rival failure. This was certainly true when Matthias and Justus drew lots nineteen centuries ago. It was coincidence rather than superior ability which gave Matthias the advantage he enjoyed for the rest of his days. It was bad luck rather than actual inferiority which sent Justus home defeated.

The same story repeats itself incessantly in modern life. Some years ago an inventor designed a new type of disc for use in the clutch of a certain automobile. The disc contained several cork inserts, and it was necessary for the inventor to devise a machine which would thrust the corks into the holes. The machine was finally built, but for some inexplicable reason it failed to work properly. After many fruitless efforts to correct the difficulty, the inventor decided to scrap the machine and devise a new model. Just before the machine was taken apart and thrown on the junk pile, a machinist carelessly left an oil can on it. The vibration of the machine upset the oil can, and the oil began to drip onto the corks as they were being inserted into successive discs. When, a few moments later, the inventor returned to dismantle the machine he found it working perfectly. All that had been needed to transform the machine from a failure into a success, the inventor from a disappointed man into a victorious one, was a drop of oil on each cork. The oil was provided by sheer accident, and thanks to that bit of luck the inventor's fame and fortune were secure. Our world to-day is full of people who, like Matthias and that inventor, have been given their victories by coincidence. It is also full of people who, like Justus and the inventors who have not had the assistance of a friendly oil can, have been accidentally sentenced to defeat. No one pretends there is any fairness to this arrangement. But that it is the existing arrangement, that an element of chance runs through human affairs, no observant person can deny.

Why is it important for all of us to remember this fact? Because, in many emergencies, this recollection will restore our waning self-confidence and our crumbling morale. If a man makes the mistake of holding himself personally responsible for everything that happens to him, a series of defeats—some deserved, and some undeserved

—will drive him to the conclusion that he is either stupid or ineffective. That false belief is certain to have serious consequences in his inner life. If, on the other hand, a man is wise enough to remind himself that many factors enter into life's situations and that sometimes (though not always) coincidence is responsible for our defeats, he will be able in a disappointing situation to retain his courage and his hope, and spur himself to confident and vigorous efforts in the future. Perhaps the next oil can that brings fame and fortune will be upset on *his* machine. Perhaps the next time lots are drawn Justus rather than Matthias will be the lucky man.

IV

Let us also remind ourselves, when we are forced to face defeat, that life is constantly bringing fresh opportunities to us all. This is a fact which disappointed people, particularly if they are people who work intensely and suffer deeply, often forget. Such individuals throw themselves with abandon into the task at hand, concentrate all their energy and all their interest on that one project, and then if it miscarries tell themselves bitterly that there is nothing left to live for. But there is always something left to live for. Life is always bringing each of us fresh opportunities. Some of them may seem small, but like the tiny door in the fairy tale they offer entrance to a world of immensity and splendor.

One day in 1916 two men who were long past youth found themselves in the same desolate boarding house at Saranac Lake. Each was the victim of tuberculosis, and each had been told by his physician that an active life—even in the favorable environment of the Adirondacks—would never be possible again. There the two men lay, hopelessly stricken by an incurable ailment. How could opportunity ever come to them? One day they decided to undertake an ingenious venture. They determined to read all the books and pamphlets within reach, copy the passages that spoke of courage and good cheer, print those quotations in an attractive pamphlet, and then mail the pamphlet far and wide. Some people would probably return a little money in payment. If enough money came back the two editors would print another pamphlet, and mail it to those who had paid for the first. In one of Charles Dickens' stories these men found the account of a quaint individual named Trotty Veck who earned his living by carrying messages, and who prided himself on being a purveyor of cheerfulness as well as information. His was the name they gave their little pamphlet, and his was the odd picture they printed on the cover. The first of the *Trotty Veck Messages* was printed in the spring of 1916, and within a year four thousand copies of that pamphlet and successive ones had been distributed. Within ten years the circulation had reached a total of more than one hundred and fifty thousand. Meantime one of the two editors had died, but the other bravely carried on. When he first went to Saranac many people thought life would never give him another opportunity, and that there was nothing left for him to do but wait stoically for death. As a matter of fact life brought him, even though he was isolated in the Adirondacks, one of the greatest opportunities imaginable—the opportunity of spreading cheer and courage to every corner of the English-speaking world. [4] Here is one of the poems he included in *Trotty Veck Message No. 20,* published in October 1931.

One broken dream is not the end of dreaming,
One shattered hope is not the end of all,
Beyond the storm and tempest stars are gleaming,
Still build your castles, though your castles fall.
Though many dreams come tumbling in disaster,
And pain and heartache meet you down the years,
Still keep your faith, your dreams and hopes to
            master,
And seek to find the lesson of your tears. [5]

Only one opportunity in life? To men who keep their courage opportunities come incessantly, down to the very end of life's strange journey.

V

There is one other fact which has brought great encouragement to many of us. We have learned that a man can be happy, wonderfully happy, even if he never wins a prize. Justus may be defeated in his first competition with Matthias, and he may

[4] See *The Knickerbocker Press* (Albany, N. Y.), December 23, 1925.
[5] Edgar Guest, "Dreams."

be defeated again every time the lots are drawn. But Justus can still find happiness. He can find it because the true sources of happiness lie outside the boundary of conventional success, and beyond the clutch of conventional failure.

This is a truth which modern Americans greatly need to hear. In recent years hundreds of well-meaning but misinformed individuals have been preaching the so-called gospel of success. By success most of them have meant—quite obviously—a large salary, a luxurious home in a good neighborhood, a social position which is the envy of everyone, and freedom from all hardship and responsibility. There, these apostles of prosperity maintain, is success—success worth talking about. Some of these modern evangelists have written books which tell people how to acquire a compelling personality, how to make themselves socially irresistible, and how to utilize the power of prayer to increase their income. The result of this widespread and prolonged success-propaganda is that America to-day is filled with people—particularly young people—who think success, plan success, and dream success; and who unfortunately define success in terms of money, real estate, social position, and release from effort. It was to such individuals that one of the contemporary exponents of prosperity recently addressed this almost incredible appeal. "By not listening in 1923 to The Silence Which Creates I lost an opportunity to make $22,000. But by heeding, during the next two years, that Silence I increased my net equity in several parcels of real estate 300%. You can do as well. For instructions remit $4.68." [6]

What now is the actual situation in the modern world? There is no possible way by which all of us can become rich. Not matter how persistently and how ingeniously we tinker with the economic machine most of us will continue to have small incomes. There is certainly no way by which all of us can acquire a home in New York and a country estate on Long Island. Most of us will continue to live in small communities, and continue to do our work among surroundings which are far from ideal. Neither can all of us achieve

[6] See Charles W. Ferguson, *The Confusion of Tongues,* p. 177.

world fame. Life gives most of us only a small
circle of friends, a limited sphere of influence, and
a reputation which extends only to the borders of
our home town. Yet even if we cannot win the
spectacular and external success on which so many
of our contemporaries have set their hearts, all of
us can be happy—wonderfully happy. We can be
happy because the sources of true happiness lie in
fields far removed from those of conventional success. Happiness grows out of friendships, out of
work well done, out of fine and interesting
thoughts, and out of a clear conscience. These are
the sources of true happiness, and they always lie
open to us all—irrespective of our wealth, the
location of our home, or the extent of our fame.
To these sources you and I can turn at any time,
whether life has assigned us the rôle of fortunate
and famous Matthias or that of unlucky and insignificant Justus. From these sources we can draw,
as Jesus did, the peace that passes understanding,
the inward joy which outward success cannot create and which outward failure can certainly never
destroy.

You have been compelled, ever since you

can remember, to watch the other person win? But that experience, hard as it is, need not embitter you or rob you of happiness. There is a profound difference between winning success outwardly and being a success inwardly. It is the second achievement which brings lasting joy, and that second achievement is always within reach of us all.

CHAPTER IX

MAINTAINING ONE'S COMPOSURE

I

In a recent volume Bruce Barton reports this incident from the life of Abraham Lincoln.[1] "In the early months of the Civil War, when no one in Washington knew how soon Lee's troops might reach the city, Lincoln and a member of his Cabinet went to call on General McClellan. Official etiquette prescribes that the President shall not call upon a private citizen, but the times were too tense for etiquette. Lincoln wanted first-hand information from the one man in Washington who could give it. The General was not at home, and for an hour the two men waited in his parlor. Finally they heard him at the door, and supposed, of course, that he would speak to them immediately. But without a word he hurried upstairs. They waited again—ten minutes, twenty, thirty.

[1] See Bruce Barton, *The Man Nobody Knows*, pp. 6, 7.

Finally Lincoln asked one of the servants to remind the General that his visitors were still waiting. Presently the servant returned, and with obvious embarrassment reported that McClellan said he was too tired to see the President. As a matter of fact he had already undressed and gone to bed. When the two men were outside the house the Cabinet member exploded in anger. Would not Lincoln instantly oust McClellan from command? But the President laid his hand quietly on the other man's shouder. 'There, there,' he said, 'don't take it so hard. I'll hold McClellan's horse if he will only bring us victories.' " What was the quality Lincoln revealed in that trying situation? One of the most valuable qualities in the world. The ability to maintain one's composure.

All great men possess this ability. Ordinary individuals fret and fume when irritating situations arise, and give a sorry display of wounded feelings when they meet snubs or unfair criticism. But great men act differently. One who watches them on such occasions sees few if any evidences of outward annoyance or inward distress. Jesus was a person of this type. The gospels report three instances of his unusual poise. The first comes from an unnamed town in Galilee.[2] A little girl had fainted, repeated efforts to revive her had failed, and finally her relatives—becoming hysterical—began to prophesy she would soon be dead. Jesus was summoned, and promptly suggested that the excited relatives leave the house. Then he entered the little girl's room quietly, gradually revived her, and wisely advised her parents to give her something to eat. What a contrast between Jesus' unruffled composure and the hysteria and helplessness of the people about him!

The other two incidents reported in the gospels are quite as suggestive. One afternoon, when Jesus and his disciples were on the road to Jerusalem, he sent two of them ahead to request overnight hospitality at a certain Samaritan village.[3] Unfortunately the ancient hostility between Jews and Samaritans flared up, the villagers refused to give Jesus and his followers shelter, and the two messengers returned in mingled chagrin and indig-

[2] Mark v. 21-24, 35-43.   [3] Luke ix. 51-56.

nation. When James and John heard what had happened they angrily proposed summoning fire from heaven to destroy the churlish Samaritans. But Jesus quietly reminded them they did not realize what they were suggesting, and then led the way in silence to the next village. The climactic evidence of Jesus' composure, however, appears in the account of the crucifixion.[4] As the Roman soldiers were nailing him to the cross he was heard to pray, "Father, forgive! They know not what they do." A recent commentator on the gospels writes,[5] "This noble saying is inconceivable under such terrible circumstances." It would be inconceivable had you or I been in Jesus' place. But what if Jesus, like so many great men before and since, had a better-than-average self-mastery? What if the superb composure which he had revealed on many lesser occasions emerged again in this supreme ordeal?

In many callings in the modern world this quality of emotional poise is frankly indispensable.

[4] Luke xxiii. 33, 34.
[5] Joseph Klausner, *Jesus of Nazareth,* p. 352.

Consider the situation in the medical profession. Who would continue to employ a doctor who, in moments of emergency or crisis, gave repeated evidences of uncertainty and confusion? Addressing the graduating class at one of our medical schools some years ago Dr. William Osler made this significant statement.[6] "In the physician or surgeon no quality takes rank with imperturbability. By it we mean presence of mind under all circumstances, calmness amid storm, clearness of judgment in moments of great peril. The physician who has the misfortune to betray indecision or anxiety, or who shows in an emergency that he is flustered and flurried, rapidly loses the confidence of his patients." Men in public life, particularly men who hold political positions, have an equal need for imperturbability. During his term as President George Washington complained that his political enemies were speaking of him "in terms so exaggerated and indecent that they could scarcely be applied to a Nero, a notorious defaulter, or even a common pickpocket." Political

[6] See William Osler, *Aequanimitas with Other Addresses,* p. 3-11.

practices seem to have changed little since that day. Unless a man can remain undisturbed when he hears himself misquoted, misrepresented, and publicly abused he had better not seek public office. Hostility and criticism on the part of his rivals are inevitable. An unruffled composure on his part is indispensable.

In the higher positions of the business world the need for emotional poise is quite as great. What is the task confronting the men and women in executive positions of major importance? They must deal day after day with a host of touchy subordinates and jealous competitors, and also with a general public which repeatedly demands the impossible. The subordinates must be kept contented and happy as well as busy, the competitors must be kept friendly or at least not hostile, and the general public must never be irritated no matter how exorbitant its expectations may be. How can bank presidents, office managers, factory executives, and heads of departments do all this, and do it year after year with no lapses of self-control, unless they possess an unusual emotional poise?

II

Anyone who studies composure carefully will soon realize that the acquisition of an unruffled poise is not the work of a few moments or even a few days. Those of us who seek emotional self-mastery must undertake a long and patient self-discipline, one which will gradually modify not only our actions in moments of crisis but also our habitual attitudes toward life and people. The first step in this long self-discipline is to teach ourselves not to expect too much from life. A certain amount of friction and a certain number of disappointments are inevitable, and we make our first advance toward composure when we recognize this fact and adjust our expectations and our emotional attitudes accordingly.

A few years ago an American traveler, trying to return from Paris to New York, met an almost incredible succession of mishaps. His difficulties began when the hotelkeeper in Paris made a mistake on his bill. A great deal of precious time was wasted correcting the blunder, and when the account was finally settled the American had just time enough to reach the station and catch the boat train for Cherbourg. As he dashed out of the hotel he collided with a workman who, as bad luck would have it, was carrying a pail of paint. When the American picked himself up, none of the paint was left in the pail and all of it was on his clothes. There was nothing to do but return to the hotel, change his suit, and miss the boat train. Half an hour later he emerged from the hotel with less speed and greater safety, and hired a taxicab to drive him to Cherbourg. A few miles outside Paris the machine broke down, and the luckless American was compelled to return once more to his starting point. By this time his only hope of reaching the boat lay in making connections by airplane, and he hurriedly wired the captain that he would try to overtake the vessel at Queenstown. He then drove at top speed to the Paris airport and crossed the Channel by plane. When the plane was over England, however, engine trouble developed, and the pilot was obliged to make an emergency landing in a field ten miles south of Croyden. After hurrying through the field and across country the American eventually caught a train for London, and there transferred to a train for Holyhead. There he caught the night boat for Ireland, and after four more changes in Ireland finally neared Queenstown. But once again bad luck intervened. He reached the dock in Queenstown just in time to see the tender, bearing the last passengers for the ship, moving relentlessly down the harbor. There were no motor boats for rent in the vicinity, and in despair the unlucky traveler hired four sturdy Irishmen to row him in a dory to the distant liner. Thanks to their superhuman efforts, induced by a colossal fee, the American finally reached the ship just as the captain was giving the order to sail. A minute after he was on board the propellers began to turn.

We smile at that story of reiterated mishaps, and yet is it not a picture of life? All of us constantly meet unexpected barriers and unforeseen difficulties. We are compelled to readjust not only our procedures but also our objectives. Finding we cannot reach our ship in conventional fashion at Cherbourg, we bend every effort to make undignified and last-minute connections at Queenstown. The beginning of wisdom, and the beginning of emotional poise, lie in recognizing these facts and teaching ourselves not to expect that every task will be easy or every venture successful. When we adopt this attitude and cease demanding the impossible from life, the unexpected misfortunes which are sure to come lose their power to surprise and annoy us. Like experienced travelers we gain the ability to complete a hazardous and a trying journey without exhibitions of irritation and anger.

It is equally important not to expect too much from other people. What are the actual facts about the men and women with whom we live and work? To begin with, many of them are in poor health—either physically or nervously. Being in poor health they often do unpredictable and erratic things, and on many occasions fail to measure up to our reasonable expectations. Furthermore, many of these people have had an inadequate education. Being uninformed or misinformed, they occasionally make unfortunate misstatements and commit serious blunders. Still again, many of these people are upset emotionally. Some of them are the victims of fear, others are plagued by unfulfilled desire, and still others are tortured by jealousy. Burdened by these difficulties they repeatedly sink below their own best level. Most significant of all, many of the individuals about us are immature. Some of them, young in years, we call children. If we are wise we disregard the unfortunate things they say and the erratic things they do. Some of them, old in years but immature intellectually and emotionally, are quite as untrustworthy in their opinions and quite as unpredictable in their actions. If we understand human nature and its vagaries we disregard the statements and the conduct of these undeveloped adults just as we disregard the statements and the conduct of youngsters. Such is the human environment in which all of us, however wise and however thoughtful we may be, live and work. The wonder is not that the men and women about us do so many strange and unfortunate things. The wonder is that, considering their handicaps, they do so many things that are wise and kindly. By recognizing this situation and deliberately scaling down both our demands and our expectations, we increase our ability to live quietly and easily. We have already mentioned the statement about imperturbability which Dr. Osler made to a group of American medical students. The concrete advice with which he concluded his address was highly valuable.[7] "One way to gain imperturbability is not to expect too much from the people amongst whom you dwell. In matters medical the average citizen to-day has not one whit more sense than the Romans of long ago. Deal gently, therefore, with this deliciously credulous human nature! Restrain your indignation when you find your pet parson carrying a bottle of sugar pills in his pocket, or when you accidentally discover a case of patent medicine in the bedroom of your best patient. It must needs be that offenses of this kind come. Expect them, and do not be vexed by them."

III

Granted that these are the first steps toward composure. What are the next steps? When an irritating situation actually arises what can we do to reëstablish our emotional balance?

[7] William Osler, *op. cit.*

Some of us have found great help by recalling this fact. In moments of stress and strain our difficulties invariably look greater than they actually are. Loss of perspective is one of the first effects of an emotional upset. Have you ever talked with a man who has just finished what he regards as an unsuccessful speech? He says bitterly that everyone in the audience noticed his two slips in grammar, that everyone realized he forgot his best illustration, and that everyone saw that his necktie was askew. As a matter of fact not one person in the audience noticed all three of these things, and only a few people noticed even one of them. The speaker was far more conscious of his difficulties than his audience was, and his shortcomings seemed far more serious to him than they did to the people who were listening to him. As a matter of fact most of those who heard his speech were oblivious of his limitations, and many of the listeners felt that his efforts were highly successful.

When we meet unfair criticism and unjust abuse we should recall this same fact. The situation, admittedly trying, seems far more serious than it actually is. Two generations ago an excited Bostonian called on Dr. Edward Everett to ask advice. One of the local papers had published an article about this man, an article which was untrue and misleading. What should the man do? Should he write an irate rejoinder and demand it be published? Or should he institute legal proceedings immediately? Dr. Everett listened patiently, and then made this quiet reply. "My dear sir, do nothing. Half the people who buy that paper never saw the article about you. Half the people who did see it failed to read it. Half of those who read it failed to understand it. Half of those who understood it knew you and refused to believe it. Half of those who believed it were people of no consequence anyway." How true those words were! They have helped many men of later days quite as much as they helped the man who first heard them.

We can also steady ourselves in moments of stress by remembering that any single experience, however disconcerting at the moment, fills only a small space in an entire lifetime. This is a fact which hysterical individuals almost invariably forget. They assure their doctor, their minister, the friend to whom they are confiding their trouble, that life can never be again what it was in the happy past. They can never survive the present disaster, never live down the present disgrace, never recover from the present failure, and never rebuild the reputation which gossip and calumny have wrecked. But these excited opinions and conclusions are far from the truth. They represent the distorted perspective of a mind which is temporarily upset by despair, shame, and fear. Look back five years in your own life. At that time you had anxieties quite as bitter as those which are troubling you to-day, and regrets quite as keen as those which now perplex you. But, strangely enough, those earlier anxieties and regrets have vanished. They have slipped into the oblivion of a thousand forgotten yesterdays, and now—no matter how vigorously you cudgel your memory—you cannot remember what they were. Standing five years beyond them you realize what an insignificant place they filled in the sweep of your life. Why not recognize that the difficulties which seem so enormous to-day will also dwindle, and finally become too small even to remember?

Once in Persia lived a king
Who upon his signet-ring
Graved a maxim true and wise
Which, if held before his eyes,
Gave him wisdom at a glance
Fit for every change and chance.
Helpful words—and these are they:
"Even this shall pass away." [8]

There is a third rule which many of us find extremely valuable in periods of tension and difficulty. Never let bitter or apprehensive feelings accumulate within your life. Rid yourself of them as fast as they emerge. Why is this constant purging of the mind so essential? Because if tensions accumulate they eventually become too powerful to control, and an emotional explosion ensues. Dr. Hadfield, one of the leading psychologists of London, gives this illustration.[9] "If, as I am riding on the train, the conductor steps on my foot it is a natural and a normal thing for me to be angry. The important question is what I do with that emotion. If I try to repress it entirely, try to pretend to myself that I am not angry, and try

[8] Theodore Tilton in *The World's Great Religious Poetry*, p. 598.
[9] See J. A. Hadfield, *Psychology and Morals*, pp. 191-2.

to assure myself that it is impossible for such a noble individual as I am to feel anger, I merely succeed in creating within myself a dangerous emotional tension. When I am at home that evening the likelihood is that my repressed ill-temper will finally and suddenly flare out, and that my wife will be the victim of the outburst." Those of us who have watched ourselves carefully know how much truth there is in this statement. If, beset by successive anxieties during a long and wearing day, we permit the sense of fear to build itself up within us, the likelihood is that our emotions will be unmanageable when night comes. As a result we shall find it almost impossible to put ourselves to sleep. If, as we go through the years, we permit ourselves to accumulate grudges toward the individuals who have wronged us, the chances are we shall eventually pay in physical or emotional ill-health for our failure to do what so many great men have repeatedly urged us to do— forgive and forget. The man who permits dangerous emotions to accumulate in the secret corners of his inner life faces the almost certain tragedy of an ultimate explosion. Only those individuals

who rid themselves of emotional tensions as fast
as these tensions arise gain the ability to live a
quiet and a steady life.

How do we rid ourselves of these tensions?
Thanks to the researches of many psychologists
the answer to that question is now clear. First
we must admit to ourselves that the emotional
tensions are actually there. When the conductor
steps on our foot we must admit to ourselves that
we are angry, thoroughly angry. But then we
must remind ourselves that a quarrel with the
conductor will bring no relief to our aching foot,
and that under the circumstances the best thing
to do is accept the conductor's apology and put
the entire incident out of the mind. When successive fears make their attack upon us we should
admit to ourselves that we are afraid, but then
follow this admission by reminding ourselves that
a day of apprehension and a night of sleeplessness
will not disclose the way out of our difficulties.
When irritating people annoy us—and what one
of us does not meet such annoyance?—we should
confess to ourselves that we are resentful, but
then face the fact that the development of a per-

manent grudge will not make the individuals who antagonize us any less irritating. In all these situations the wise thing to do is put the annoying experience completely out of the mind, and continue putting it out of the mind no matter how many times it recurs. Jesus called this act "forgiving seventy times seven," and from that day to this teachers and preachers have taken his suggestion, rephrased it in the language of their community and their generation, and then offered it again to the world.

> If an unkind word appears
> File the thing away,
> If some novelty in jeers
> File the thing away,
> If some clever little bit
> Of a sharp and pointed wit
> Carrying a sting with it,
> File the thing away.
> Do this for a little while
> Then go out and burn the file.[10]

What is this but Jesus' advice, phrased in the language and imagery of a commercial age?

Our final suggestion will undoubtedly seem

[10] See *The World's Famous Short Poems*, p. 133.

strange and unconvincing to some people, but to others it will prove the most helpful of all. Behind it is the authority of centuries of human experience, in the non-Christian as well as the Christian world. As we struggle to maintain our inward poise let us remember that multitudes of people have gained immense help from the habit of prayer. Obviously the forms of prayer vary greatly. Some individuals pray by repeating sentences memorized long ago. Others pray by addressing God in brief phrases of their own quick devising. Still others—and many of us belong in this final group—pray by growing inwardly quiet and deliberately focusing the mind on the reality, the nearness, and the unfailing love of God. But all these people gain immediate and immense help from the act of prayer. Jesus' words, "Everyone that asketh receiveth, everyone that seeketh findeth, to everyone that knocketh it shall be opened," [11] prove profoundly and permanently true.

What is the explanation of the benefit which thus comes, generation after generation, to so

[11] Matthew vii. 8.

many people? Part of the help accruing from the habit of prayer is traceable to the fact that the act of praying changes the focus of a man's attention and by so doing tends to rest the mind. Part of the help is traceable to the fact that sincere prayer almost invariably involves an element of beneficial auto-suggestion. But, so some of us believe, these familiar explanations do not cover all the facts in the case. We believe that when men open their hearts in their own way to the all-encompassing God, His help—like silent, invading sunlight—flows steadily in. This help comes, not as a change miraculously precipitated in the external situation, but as a change quietly wrought within the inner life of the man who prays. New ideas and ideals are given him by God, and from these new ideas and ideals there gradually emerge the new courage, the new wisdom, the new endurance, and the new composure which the man desperately needs. These are not the speculations of a little group of professionally religious men. They are the daily experience of thousands of normal, intelligent people who represent many nationalities, many creeds, and many callings. To them all has come the unshaken and unshakable conviction that God does hear and answer prayer, and that He answers it by "restoring the soul" of the man who prays.

Some years ago a graduate student at one of our American universities made this significant confession.[12] "I had been separated from my wife and my children for more than a year. I felt I must continue my studies, but naturally I wanted to have my family with me. This could be arranged only in case I found a particular type of part-time work. I received a tentative offer of a position, applied in person for it, made a poor impression on my prospective employer, and finally—at the end of a particularly exhausting day—was told bluntly that I could not have the job. I shall never forget the long ride back to my room that night. It was nearly two o'clock in the morning when I finally got to bed, but I was too worried and too disappointed to sleep. The next morning I went about my studies as best I could, but finally I abandoned the effort and came

[12] See H. N. Wieman, *Religious Experience and Scientific Method,* p. 225.

back to my room to have things out with myself. I sat there alone for nearly four hours, sometimes praying and sometimes just thinking. Gradually the almost unendurable pain which possessed me began to subside, and a great courage and gladness filled my heart. The external situation remained just as tragic as it had been before, but I regained my composure and began to feel I could go ahead and take whatever came. There were no traces of hallucination or abnormality in the experience. My anguish gradually vanished, and inward peace took its place. Best of all, that peace stayed with me permanently."

We have something more than our own resources as we struggle to gain composure. Our tiny human lives, like innumerable inlets fringing the sea, open out upon the vastness and the peace of God.

CHAPTER X

MAKING A NEW START IN MIDDLE LIFE

I

Is such a thing possible? We hear to-day two entirely different answers to the question. Many people tell us that any attempt to make extensive alterations in a human personality, particularly after the age of twenty, is foredoomed to fail. Each individual has at birth, so these people say, a certain set of inherited qualities—physical, mental, and emotional. During childhood a certain habit pattern is rapidly superimposed on those native qualities, and within a surprisingly short time the contour of the self is definitely and permanently fixed. From that moment the individual is what the combination of his inheritance and his acquired habits determines he shall be. How soon does a human self thus acquire its final form? When William James discussed that question a generation ago he implied that the plastic period

217

lasted for some twenty years. Modern psychologists are not so encouraging. One expert in child training now claims that by the time a baby is four years old the pattern of his personality has been definitely established. Another expert restricts the formative period even further, and maintains that by the time the baby has reached his second birthday this pattern has taken shape. Thereafter the child's—and later the man's—thoughts, beliefs, emotions, and actions run down the secret channels unconsciously but inexorably carved for them. If this theory is true the suggestion that middle-aged men and women make a new start is almost comic. If our behavior patterns were laid down in the nursery, and if we shall always be what those behavior patterns predetermine, why try to improve ourselves at this late date?

Other people to-day, facing this same question of the possibility of radical self-change, give an entirely different answer. They assure us blandly that anything is possible—that any man can have anything he wants, and have it at any time he decides to ask for it. One individual who holds this belief writes cheerfully, "If you are sick the Holy Spirit will heal you. If you are unhappy the Holy Spirit will adjust conditions and bring about harmony. If you are in financial need the Holy Spirit will show you the way to prosperity. If your need is urgent telegraph us for instructions." Still another exponent of this doctrine makes promises which are even more alluring. "I can give you charm that will make you irresistibly popular, personal power that will amaze your friends. Don't pay me a cent if I can't give you a Magnetic Personality. Five days of proof free." [1]

Most of us, studying these rival answers to the question, feel that the truth probably lies somewhere between these two extremes. Having trained (and presumably improved) several children of our own after the magic age of two was past, we cannot believe that the habit patterns of a human personality are definitely and irrevocably laid down before the second birthday. Having tried in vain to achieve the affluence and the personal charm which are said to be immediately

[1] See C. W. Ferguson, *The Confusion of Tongues*, pp. 226 and 176.

available to everyone, we have been driven to conclude that human personalities are not so plastic as some of our optimistic contemporaries maintain. Here, as in so many instances, the true answer to the question lies between the two extremes of opinion. Have we any idea what that true answer is?

II

Long experience has shown that when an adult attempts to make a new start he encounters one or more of four fairly obvious difficulties. The first is his inheritance. His parents and grandparents passed on to him certain physical traits, and also certain qualities of mind and spirit. Sometimes the very traits he abhors were perversely given him, and sometimes the abilities he most ardently desires were unluckily omitted from his make-up. When he attempts to make a new start in middle life the venture thus involves a double effort—controlling inherited impulses which he heartily despises, and building up within himself other qualities which were originally either inadequate in scope or apparently omitted entirely. Are these efforts foredoomed to defeat, or can a man break the grip of his inheritance? Are we the creatures of heredity, or can we make ourselves better than the family record implies we will be?

The next time those questions perplex you count the number of your ancestors. Two parents, four grandparents, eight great-grandparents, sixteen great-great-grandparents, and then how swiftly the numbers jump! With every generation they double, and before long they assume fantastic proportions. In the generation which saw the *Mayflower* sail in 1620 you had, in that single generation, well over one thousand direct forbears. If you go back six centuries instead of three you will locate in the fourteenth century a generation which provided you with over two million ancestors. In the preceding generation the number was, of course, twice as great. An essayist has recently pointed out the fact [2] that in the fourteenth century the entire population of England, recently ravaged by the plague, was only about two million souls. The implication is that those of us who

[2] See Hugh Elliot, *Modern Science and Materialism*, p. 78.

can boast a purely English lineage have within ourselves to-day the commingled traits of all the people who were living in England shortly after the year 1300. Granted that our largest inheritance was provided by our parents and grandparents. It is equally true that other traits and tendencies, instincts and impulses, abilities and possibilities were provided by other ancestors further back in that shadowy, ever-widening throng. What if some of the fine traits thus passed on to us have been waiting for discovery and development? What if there are, buried deep within our heart, treasures of inherited ability which are capable of transforming what seems an ordinary self?

In June 1929 a young student from India won at Harvard University the coveted degree of Doctor of Philosophy, and promptly returned to his native land to begin teaching philosophy at one of the leading Indian universities. What is this professor's recent inheritance? As far as he can trace it, it is distinctly unimpressive. His father was a poor villager, barely literate. His paternal grandfather was even less promising as an ances-

tor. That grandfather was an outcast, one of
India's untouchables. The food he ate came to
him secondhand from some one else's table, and
the work he did was of the most menial and
degrading type. Yet the descendant from this
human stock now proves to be a man with an
extraordinary mind, a man who was able to win
one of the highest academic distinctions offered
by the modern world, and a man who occupies
a position of great distinction and wide influence
in the intellectual life of his nation.[8] How do we
explain such a situation? All we can say is that in
this case, as in the case of Shakespeare, there
must have been far back in the family line ancestors of a superior type whose abilities were preserved, passed on, and fortuitously combined in
this present-day genius.

The meaning of all this for those who in middle life quietly determine to make a new start is
plain. We have no cause to fear our inheritance.
We should not be terrified by the bugaboo of
"the family traits." What if some of our ances-

[8] Reported by the American Board of Commissioners for
Foreign Missions.

tors were unpromising? What if some of the traits passed on to us were not what we would have chosen? There are other ancestors in the vast throng behind us who gave us an inheritance of which we can be justly proud. There are qualities within our personality which can be developed and made the impressive features of a reorganized and singularly valuable self. Thousands of people, breaking free from an irrational fear of the past, have rebuilt themselves and finally attained heights of character and achievement which would once have been termed unattainable. What other men and women have done you and I can certainly do.

III

Another obstacle we encounter as we try to make a new start in middle life is the group of habits which we built, usually unconsciously, in childhood. Some of these habits are obvious, some are only partially evident, and some elude our observation entirely. But for good or for ill all of them influence our thoughts and our actions incessantly. As psychologists now agree we become, by the time we reach maturity, "bundles of habits." Do these habits dominate and predetermine everything we do, or is there a way by which we can control within limits their silent but persistent power?

The answer to that question is more obvious than many people think. You and I cannot annihilate old habits, but we can always start building new ones. In our power to build new habits, and by means of these new habits gradually counteract the power of old ones, lies our power to manage ourselves and determine our future development. If you study the record of human life you soon realize that this process of building new habits and thus breaking the grip of old ones is going on all the time. The act we call "taking a lesson"—whether it is in golf, good manners, or the art of thinking logically—is nothing more nor less than the act of building a new habit which, slowly superimposed on an old one, gradually alters the mechanism of conduct and changes the future development of the self. A violin teacher tells us that our tone will be better if we press the strings more firmly against the finger board of our instrument, and move the right wrist more flexibly in the process of bowing. We practice in the new way for a month, a year, or a decade, and finally the full, smooth tone we always wanted is ours. The old habit is obliterated by the new one, and we find ourselves playing the violin more acceptably than we ever did in the past. The way of escape from bad habits is surprisingly obvious. It is to build good habits. And the thing which gives middle-aged people hope and confidence is the fact that this habit-building process can be undertaken at any time.

Sometimes the emancipation thus attained by an intelligent and a determined adult almost passes belief. A generation ago a boy in Baltimore resolved to make himself a tennis champion. He had genuine ability as a tennis player, and for a time it seemed as if he would speedily realize his ambition. But one day in 1919 tragedy intervened. While he was hunting, an explosion of his gun blew off his entire right arm at the shoulder. How could a man with only one arm, and that the wrong arm, ever win a tennis championship? But with indomitable courage that crippled athlete set out to build a new set of tennis habits. After years of persistent practice he learned to hold both the ball and the racket in his left hand, fling the ball high into the air, and then during its descent regain such a grip on the racket that he could make a powerful serve. A decade of struggle, and then in 1929 this one-armed player actually won the national title for veterans in tournament play at Forest Hills, Long Island. He was then forty-five years old, he had only one arm, and that was the wrong one. Yet he won his championship at last. How did he do it? By building a new set of habits.

The same process goes on in the realm of character reconstruction. Men and women who were once hot-tempered, intolerant, and critical slowly cultivate habits of self-control, open-mindedness, and friendly judgment of others. Individuals who were once habitually depressed and depressing gradually make themselves cheerful, optimistic, and inspiring to their friends. There is no magic in this process. It represents merely the stubborn and persistent effort to create a new set of habits and superimpose it on an old. A generation ago

Lafcadio Hearne, the European who became a naturalized Japanese, wrote in a letter this interesting description of his native servant.[4] "My Japanese cook always wears a smiling, healthy, pleasing face. He is decidedly a good-looking young man. But one day I happened to glance through the hole in the partition and saw him when he was sitting alone in the kitchen. The face was not the same at all. It was thin and drawn, and showed queer lines worn by old hardships. But when I went to speak to him he suddenly changed, and became young and attractive once more. My cook wears a mask of happiness as part of his etiquette." What a picture of the struggle to build new habits and lay them patiently and permanently over the old!

IV

The third obstacle many middle-aged people encounter as they try to make a new start is an unfriendly environment. Repeatedly the world in which we live seems determined to thwart our

[4] See Karl De Schweinitz, *The Art of Helping People Out of Trouble*, p. 1.

efforts at self-emancipation and self-development. Repeatedly it seems to show a vicious intention to keep us what we are, maintain within us the very qualities we are seeking to eliminate. If our environment were inspiring and encouraging the problem of making a new start would be greatly simplified. But when our environment seems determined to thwart our new start can we possibly succeed in beginning anew? This was evidently one of Jesus' problems. Nazareth was not an ideal place in which to live. Jesus' associates were certainly not stimulating people. Jesus' family seems to have been, if we can trust the record of the earliest gospel, a hindrance rather than a help. It was in this unfriendly and uninspiring environment that Jesus had to live, think, and work. When he spoke of the sycamine tree that grew in the ocean [5] was he, as Dr. Coffin suggests, thinking of himself? This was Jesus' problem— trying to be one thing when his environment seemed determined to make him another. When you and I find ourselves confronted by this difficulty can we hope to conquer it?

[5] Luke xvii. 6.

The best answer to that question is the actual record of human life. Jesus built a matchless personality and gained an unrivaled insight into truth, though he had to do these things against the background of first-century Nazareth and amid the baffling obstacles which ignorance, jealousy, and spite created. Abraham Lincoln's early home left a great deal to be desired. Who would imagine that out of a backwoods cabin in Kentucky would come the most impressive personality America has yet produced? In the modern world the same story of triumph over environment repeats itself endlessly. Study the letter which Robert Louis Stevenson wrote George Meredith in 1893. "For fourteen years I have not had a day of real health. I have wakened sick, and gone to bed weary. I have written my books in bed and out of bed, written them between hemorrhages, written them when I was torn by coughing, written them when my head swam for weakness. I have done this for so long that it seems to me I have now won my wager and recovered my glove. But the battle still goes on—ill or well is a trifle so long as it goes. I was made for a contest, and the Powers That Be have willed that my battle-field shall be the dingy, inglorious one of the bed and the medicine-bottle." What were the books that came out of that desolating environment? Stories of brave adventure that delight the heart of boyhood. Gay poems that bring laughter into the eyes of little children. Essays on courage and cheerfulness which make healthy individuals ashamed of their self-pity and their all-too-frequent whining.

> If I have faltered more or less
> In my great task of happiness . . .

So sang this brave man, dying of tuberculosis. His record, and the records of a thousand indomitable men like him, are a proof that an unfriendly environment is nothing to fear. A man who is thoroughly in earnest about making a new start can make one, no matter how drab and discouraging is the world in which he finds himself, and against which he must struggle incessantly.

V

The final obstacle we meet as we try to make a new start is the one which, curiously enough, disturbs middle-aged people most. It is the number of our birthdays. Many adults are ready to confess that if they were still in their teens, or if they were even in the early twenties, they might rearrange their inherited traits, build new and more valuable habits, and overcome the downward tug of an uninspiring environment. But as they count the years that are gone they tell themselves disconsolately that this project of reconstructing the self must be left to those who are younger and presumably more plastic. "An old dog cannot learn new tricks" these middle-aged pessimists murmur sadly, and then—picturing themselves as old dogs—they settle down to a dreary acceptance of a personality, a career, and an achievement which are admittedly unsatisfactory. But is age a hopeless handicap? Are old dogs as incapable of education as the familiar maxim states?

Recently Professor Thorndike of Columbia University devised a series of experiments designed to test the learning ability of people who are frankly past youth.[6] He divided the four

[6] See Edward L. Thorndike, *Adult Learning* (The Macmillan Company).

hundred and sixty-five students in his classes at Teachers College into three groups—the first made up of those who were still in the twenties, the second made up of those in the thirties, and the third made up of those who were forty years of age and over. In the actual tests which had been prepared which group would make the best showing? Would the so-called "young people" always come out ahead?

Contrary to everyone's expectation the third group, made up of those who were forty and over, showed a distinct preëminence in practically every test. Perhaps the most novel experiment was one which measured a person's ability to learn to write with the wrong hand. Would "old people" prove teachable in this regard? Repeated tests showed that after only fifteen hours of practice forty-year-olds showed as much improvement in this line as children normally show after two full years of struggle. Professor Thorndike summarized his findings in a statement which disheartened adults would do well to ponder. "We have discovered a strong array of facts indicating that mature men and women can learn almost anything they want to. Adults are plastic and teachable in every mental function. If I had to draw a general conclusion from all our findings it would be this—that the learning ability of middle-aged people is very nearly as great as that of youngsters at the highly favorable ages of seventeen, eighteen, and nineteen." Evidently the old dogs are not so badly off as they have been led to believe!

When we turn from laboratory studies to actual life we find this theory that adults can make a new start substantiated a thousand times. Young people in the teens and twenties are not the only ones who succeed in reorganizing their personality, breaking free from the past, and entering a new world of splendor. Elderly people do this too. Recently the minister of a New England church reported a striking instance of such achievement.[7] In his parish lived an elderly woman who for years had made little attempt to interest herself in outside affairs, little attempt to win and keep friends, and no attempt to control her shrewish tongue. Her younger sister, cultivating the opposite attitudes and habits, had made

[7] An incident related to the author.

a large place for herself in the life of the community, and received almost constant attention from a throng of friends. The older sister, failing to appreciate the difference between her personality and that of her sister, imagined that the people who visited the home in which the two women lived were coming there to see both of them. But after her sister's sudden death she learned the unhappy truth. Once the days which immediately followed the funeral were past, not a soul came to call. Day after day the lonely elder sister waited in the silent home, but the door bell never rang. Evidently all the callers had come to visit the younger sister. Evidently the older sister did not have a friend in the world. Finally, in spite of the fact this woman was in her eighty-ninth year, she determined she would change this doleful situation. She resolved to make herself as friendly and attractive as her sister had been, win as many friends as her sister had won. Despite the handicap of extreme age and the handicap of a well-established reputation for shrewishness, this woman of eighty-nine actually succeeded in her efforts. Within a year people far and near were remarking on her newly acquired kindness, tolerance, and patience, and callers began to appear again at her door. The local minister summed up the story in a highly encouraging sentence. "This old lady was actually converted, and converted when she was almost ninety." Old age an insuperable barrier? Nothing of the kind. As this story shows, it is never too late to begin again.

VI

All this brings us face to face with one of the great messages of Christianity. We Christians are convinced that when a man, no matter how old or how handicapped he is, plucks up courage to make a new start help comes to him from a source outside himself—from a living, loving God. What is the help which God gives? Obviously it is not a change in the man's surroundings, or a miraculous elimination of his personal difficulties. The outside situation remains exactly what it was before, and the inward forces arrayed against the man are still as vicious and as powerful as they were in the past. But God changes the man himself, changes him by thrusting new ideas and new ideals into his mind. The man suddenly realizes that life still holds glorious possibilities for him, that he possesses the same power which other people have displayed, and that as he utilizes to the full his own energies they will be steadied and reinforced by continuous help from God. These convictions re-create the man's inner life. He finds himself brave rather than dispirited, hopeful rather than depressed, confident rather than timorous. Presently he goes out to solve his own problems and win his own battles, literally remade by the power of God. God might give us victory in life by fighting and wining our battles for us. Instead He gives us victory by making us able to fight and win those battles ourselves. Is not the divine help as real, the divine reinforcement as significant, in the second case as it would be in the first?

How do we get the help God has for us? There is only one way. By deliberately undertaking the long, hard struggle with ourselves. This resolute effort at self-mastery opens the secret doorways of the spirit, and then God's help—always wait-

ing outside every human heart—flows quietly and
steadily in.

It will do no good to lie.
    Hold your eyelids wide, look straight.
Stare, stare, nor deny
    The hard, dim thing you hate.

This is you, alone and old.
    Yes, she has no loveliness.
Yes, she stumbles and is cold
    In that thick, black dress.

Say not: She is none of mine,
    Husk of a life, unloved, unknown
Stare, stare, learn each line
    Of fading for your own.

You who sit behind the eyes
    Juggling life and judging death,
Too immortal and too wise
    To fail with failing breath,

Soul, soul, voyager
    Of wild, unclaimed eternity,
Face her! Never pity her!
    You alone can set her free.[8]

[8] From Fannie Stearns Davis Gifford, *The Ancient Beautiful Things*. By permission of The Macmillan Company, publishers.